RESTORING MY FATHER'S HONOR
A SON'S CRUSADE

DAVID E. STANLEY

I8E

Los Angeles | Nashville

Copyright ©2015 by Impello Entertainment

All rights reserved under international and Pan-American copyright conventions. No part of this work may be reproduced or transmitted in any form by any means, electronic or mechanical, including photocopying and recording, or by any information storage or retrieval system as may be expressly permitted by the 1976 Copyright Act or as expressly permitted in writing by the publisher.

Impello Entertainment

1222 16th Avenue South – Suite 10 Nashville, TN. 37212

info@impelloentertainment.com

Printed in the United States of America

First Edition Printing 2015

ISBN 9780996666725

Edited by Nikki Edwards

Other Works by David E. Stanley

Conversations with the King: Journals of a Young Apprentice

Raised on Rock: Growing Up at Graceland

The Elvis Encyclopedia

Coming Soon to a Book Store Near You

Growing Up Graceland

Predator in the Pulpit

Coming Soon to a Theatre Near You

Restoring My Father's Honor: A Son's Crusade

Growing Up Graceland

Author's Note

This book is a true story based on the compilation of the memoirs and recollections of my father, Sgt. William J. Stanley, my mother, Dee Stanley-Presley, my stepfather Vernon Presley, my stepbrother Elvis Presley, and my life long friends Lamar Fike and Red West as to the events that took place in Germany from 1958-1960 while my family was stationed in Germany. As I was only a toddler when these events unfolded, I have relied on their memories and interpretations of the past to pull together the truth of what really happened to my father.

To my father, Master Sgt. William J. Stanley, a true American Hero.

Acknowledgements

To my elder brothers, Billy and Ricky Stanley—we were on this journey together, and this book would have never been possible without the two of you.

To my sons, Austin and Tyler Stanley—so you may both know the truth about your grandfather and eternally honor him.

To my beloved mother, Dee Stanley-Presley—thank you for doing what you thought was best, and always putting your boys first.

To my stepbrother Elvis Presley—thank you for becoming the father that I lost, and for always encouraging me to honor my father.

To Lynn Stanley – Thank you for your encouragement, love and prayers through all the years. We did it Lynn.

To my late friend Lamar Fike—thank you for believing in me and this story from the beginning.

To Nikki Edwards—thank you for helping me move the story from thoughts in my head to words on a page.

To my business partner and dear friend David LaChance—thank you for supporting this project from start to finish.

To a mentor and great friend Berny Dohrmann—thank you for standing next to me for all these years and your driving force in making this book a reality.

List of Chapters

Death of a Hero
The Early Years & WWII
A New Family
A New Enemy
The Forbidden Fruit
And So It Begins
A Seed of Doubt
A Wolf in Sheep's Clothing
A Snake in the Grass
Elvis and Vernon: A Battle of Wills
Blinded by Fame
The Tactics of War
The Army Draws the Line
A Wife Abandoned
Vernon Under Fire
A Persistent Enemy
Vernon Prevails
The Ultimate Betrayal
The Spoils of War
The Carnage of War
Epilogue

DAVID E. STANLEY

Death of a Hero

"Show me a hero and I'll write you a tragedy.

F. Scott Fitzgerald

February 28, 1991 was a beautifully snowy morning at my home in Fairfax, VA as I busied myself preparing for the day. I remember hearing the shrill of the phone from the bedroom. I hurried from the bathroom, and answered the phone with a short hello.

"David," the caller said. "This is Billy. Daddy's dead. He passed away this morning."

I sat in silence for a moment as the news I had just received sank in. Billy, my older brother, asked me if I was all right. With both of us holding back tears, I said I was okay.

My dad had been sick for several months, and we both know that this day was coming soon. We also knew that he was now in a better place.

As I set the phone back in its cradle, I reflected back on our last visit 6 months prior. I was doing a speaking engagement in Edmonton, Canada when I got the call that he was very sick. I traveled all day to get to him at the hospital in Jacksonville, FL.

It had been many years since I had last seen him. When I arrived at the hospital, my two older brothers Billy and Ricky were there to meet me.

We entered his room and sat on the bed. A lifelong struggle with alcoholism had taken its toll on his body. Weak and defeated, he was a shell of his former self.

It was a tough visit for me, as I'd never really understood what had happened between he and my mom, and how he could have abandoned his boys. I was only 4 years old when I watched him drive away for the last time, and my mother never really wanted to talk about it much. All she would ever say about him was that he was a combat veteran and an alcoholic. She and my dad divorced in 1960 and she remarried—this time to Vernon Presley, father of Elvis Presley.

Though I was losing a father, I was so young that I couldn't fully comprehend what was happening. My father's loss was my gain. I had everything a boy could ever dream of—my own room, a huge yard to play in, countless toys and a doting new older stepbrother in the form of Elvis Presley.

Elvis always felt sorry for my dad and made a point of looking after me. He played with me, filled his yard full of toys, wiped my tears, attended my football games and drove me to school--all the things my dad missed out on. Even though he never spoke of what happened to me directly, he told me I should honor and respect my father in spite of the circumstances.

As the three of us sit and talked with this man we barely knew, he wept, drawing each one of us close to him to tell us how much he loved and missed us. I told him I loved him too, kissed him on the forehead and left the room. The next day I left and went back home to Virginia.

I called up my older brother Ricky, and we talked about the upcoming funeral. I didn't feel the need or the pull to attend, as I had made my peace with my dad at our last visit several months ago. Ricky warned me I would regret not attending, but he was never there for me growing up, so I decided it was best for me to move on.

Neither my brother Billy nor myself attended the funeral. Ricky did, and in my absence watched a man who was a combat veteran of WWII and the Korean War with almost 20 years serving our country be buried without honors. Not even a flag, and no 21-gun salute. It was shameful. I just shook my head and thought what a waste of a life—all of that dedication and service and it had amounted to nothing at all in the end but a pile of regret.

Several weeks passed after the service, and I received a knock at my door that would forever alter my perception of my father and his life after he left us. As I answered the door, a man stood there with a package for me. I signed for it and closed the door.

I noticed it was postmarked from Florida where my dad had lived, and I opened it with a mix of curiosity and wonder. I pulled out a rather large stack of papers—some handwritten and some typed. Unbeknownst to me, my father had painstakingly written his memoirs and left them to his boys. I was immediately curious, as my mother was always tightlipped about what had happened all those years ago, and no one else had ever really filled in the gaps.

I could never wrap my mind around the fact that he had walked away from us. The only thing that had ever made sense to me was that he couldn't handle the fact that I was a cripple. I had been born with a clubfoot and had undergone many painful surgeries by the time I was 5 years old. I was in leg braces for years, and still walk with a limp to this day. Being in and out of the hospital for surgeries, procedures and checkups was a common part of my early life, and I'd always assumed he was embarrassed of my disability, and me in particular.

It was tough growing up thinking your dad walked away because you weren't good enough. And no matter how welcoming, kind and compassionate my stepbrother Elvis Presley was to us when we arrived at Graceland in 1960, that thought still stung.

As I paged through his handwritten notes, I wondered what he would have to say for himself, and if he could ever explain leaving our lives and eventually starting a new family without us.

I walked into my den with my father's memoirs, and sat down to start reading. As I began, I had no idea the journey I was starting, and where these words would ultimately lead me. For what I had thought about my father for the entirety of my 36 years had been sorely inaccurate and negatively influenced by powerful sources.

My father had a very different story from the one that I was raised with. As I combed through the pages before me, I began to understand him and his struggles. He had been a combat solider in two wars and served his country with honor, only to lose his boys in the one battle he could never win.

Was he perfect? Absolutely not. Did he struggle with alcoholism? He certainly did. But he didn't deserve to be forgotten by a country that he dedicated his life to defending. This is his story...

The Early Years & WWII

"The cost of freedom is always high, but Americans have always paid it. And one path we shall never choose, and that is the path of surrender, or submission."

John F. Kennedy

Born on September 1, 1922, my father grew up dirt poor in North Carolina as the youngest of five kids. New clothes were unheard of, and he was lucky to have a pair of shoes to wear. Hunger was a part of daily life, and everyone he knew lived in poverty.

His father (my grandfather) was the postmaster for Brunswick County, as well as the sheriff, and worked a third job at the sawmill. He was never around, and left parenting mostly to his wife who was passive at best.

When my father was 6 years old, my grandfather was horribly disfigured in an accident at the sawmill. He lost his leg from the knee down, and my father witnessed the entire traumatic event. The accident led his father to begin drinking—and heavily. He was never the same again.

As he started school, no one really seemed to care if he actually attended or not. His father would drink all day, and would come home at 3:00am thoroughly intoxicated. He would pull my father out of bed to play checkers, and keep him up until it was time to go to school. If he fell asleep, my grandfather would poke him with his walking stick, and often beat him if he didn't respond fast enough. Consequently, he would hide in order to sleep until noon.

Growing up, my father had one friend—Vernon Teague. He spent all of his free time at Vernon's house, and it was the only time he felt like he had a real family. Vernon's mom was special, and always made him feel welcome. She fed him breakfast and packed him lunch, and made sure he didn't go hungry. She felt sorry for the little boy with an alcoholic and abusive father, and did her best to make up for it.

As he got older, my father's life became less and less stable. He avoided home as much as he could, and one by one his older siblings moved out. He eventually was sent to live with his sister Pearl, and was shuttled between homes on a weekly basis. He was often seen pushing his roll away bed from house to house carrying everything he owned in a sack.

By the time he was 14, his siblings were tired of hosting him. He was very big for his age, and could easily pass for 20. He realized he could fudge his age and get a real full time job. His father was demanding he help out if he wanted a place to live, so they picked up and moved to Baltimore to be near his oldest sister.

My father was fortunate enough to land a job in a box factory, and turned over his entire paycheck to his parents on a weekly basis. It was never enough to keep his father in wine though. Through the factory he met a guy who was in the National Guard, and decided to join. He lied about being only 15, and signed up.

The next 2 years were the best of his life. He was making money at the factory and with the National Guard, and lived for the weekends on duty. He then took a position at the Baltimore City Hospital that included living quarters, and finally felt he was doing something he loved and giving back. Though he was still giving most of his earnings back to his parents, his social life was picking up. He always made sure to keep enough money from his paychecks to take girls out to the movies or for a ride.

The hospital gave him the opportunity to learn about teamwork and gave him a sense of camaraderie. Everyone was working together for a common good, and he made friends for the first time in his teenage life. He played baseball in the park with his co-workers, and enjoyed his newly found stability.

He struggled a bit with females, and often felt inferior intellectually as education had never been a focus for him. He had always gotten by on brawn and strength instead. Matters of the heart eluded him—especially with only the troubled marriage of his own parents as an example. But all in all, he was happy and well adjusted working at the hospital and with the National Guard.

In February of 1941 his unit was mobilized into federal service. He was sent to Fort Meade in Maryland for nine months as part of the 175th Infantry Regiment, the 29th Infantry Division, which ended his job at the hospital in Baltimore. He took pride in the uniform, and was meticulous in following orders. The Army was a very serious endeavor for him, and he valued his service. This was also a time when the general public respected and revered the military, and my father flourished in this environment.

As a full time soldier, he was assigned to platoon sergeant and was determined to move up the ranks quickly. This was the opportunity he had been waiting for, and felt like he was exactly where he was supposed to be. Even though he was young, he wanted to serve his country and be the best soldier he could be.

Prior to the invasion of Hitler's fortress Europe in June of 1944, he was sent to England and then eventually on to France.

My father shared his personal account of his time in Europe in his memoirs...

Three weeks prior to our departure for Normandy, the army began pulling men with past infantry training out of a boat brigade that I had been assigned to and put us in the infantry. I was put on a landing craft where I sat for three weeks in the rain, waiting to leave. We were told nothing. I found myself trying to keep my head clear.

On June 1st, in the cold rain, with waves crashing over the deck of the boat, we sat out. It was a miserable six days. My fellow soldiers, not used to the rhythmic rocking of the sea, became seasick. The chill and dampness bit through my uniform. I was beginning to realize the severity of war, and we weren't even there yet.

The sky was dark with hundreds of bombers, and I remember the fear erupting inside me as the storm and cold played havoc on my exterior.

At three in the morning on June 6, 1944, we were offloaded to LCM crafts, about thirty-six feet long, each holding about forty men. Each of us occupied about one square foot per man and carried over 125 pounds of equipment.

We circled for one and a half hours in the storm, and then headed for the beach. One hundred feet from shore, my landing craft hit a sand bar.

Thinking we were on the beach, the coxswain dropped the ramp, which was a signal to disembark, and we ran into twelve feet of water. There was widespread panic as the weaker and non-swimmers drowned.

The war ended for them one hundred feet from the Invasion on Omaha Beach. The shock, fear, and reality of what happened are indescribable. When my feet touched the beach, I made my way to shore, stumbling and pushing bodies of my American comrades aside.

There was only one way to go-- ahead. Machine-gun fire hit the water, and bodies became sandbags and protection. Not one American son could ever be prepared for this. Everything was instinctive and I kept moving ahead.

We huddled behind the sand dunes on the beach while the artillery continued firing toward us. The choice was either to huddle there and be killed by machine-gun fire, or move forward. We regrouped and moved ahead. We gradually advanced and the beachhead was established.

After the second day, there was a lull in the fighting and divisions began reforming. We molded again into a fighting force. We were close-knit groups, and received little news about what was happening in the other areas.

We began moving ahead. I saw gliders with dead pilots and dead paratroopers hanging from trees and house roofs. We kept moving with little resistance, scared and tired. We passed through small villages, and at times were shot at by French collaborators.

After three days, we had a twelve-hour reprieve where I fell into an exhausted sleep. The weather finally had broken. The sun shone brightly, and for the first time I felt a degree of warmth. For the next three months, we moved slowly, steadily forward, fighting by day and digging in at night. Occasionally we were hit at night. I became resigned to one fact – kill or be killed. I saw buddies wounded and killed, but could not comprehend it actually happening to me.

One day it became me. While I was making a routine check of my platoon, I was hit in both knees by a burst of machine-gun fire. I was placed on a stretcher and taken by ambulance to the emergency field hospital. My legs were splinted. I was given morphine for the pain. I was awarded a Purple Heart, and thought I had the "million dollar wound" – a ticket home for sure. The war would be over for me. I was elated. I longed to see the U.S. again.

With an IV in each arm, I was moved to the field hospital on the beach. I watched chaplains comfort the wounded and dying, listened to the constant groaning of pain, day and night.

It was a frightening experience, and I longed to get out of there. Chaplains stopped by and asked if they could write my family for me. I told them there was no one to write to and to please take care of those around me.

By this time, I had been molded into a true career soldier and my buddies were my first concern.

A day or two later, I was loaded on a Navy hospital ship. I believed we were headed for the States, but we landed at Plymouth, England, where I was admitted to a military hospital. The British operated on my knees, and I recuperated for three months. The bullets were removed, and two full leg casts were applied. I recovered and eventually was allowed passes.

One of the first things I noticed was the

attitude of the British people. They had done a 100 percent turnaround from when we first arrived, and were actually friendly. This was quite refreshing after my ordeal.

I was loaded on a troop ship, still thinking I was being sent home. But we landed in Cherbourg, France, and I was reassigned to heavy boat company as captain of a large tugboat. I towed barges to ships too large to put ashore and transported cargo, and this continued until the beginning of the Battle of the Bulge.

Again, they pulled men who had infantry experience and assigned us to infantry units near Belgium. I was a platoon sergeant and back in the fighting as the Germans were throwing everything they had at us. We retaliated, slowly moving forward.

About two months prior to the end of the war, some of the veteran combat NCOs were pulled to the rear to train incoming replacements, and I was still doing this when the war ended.

The CO called a formation and announced the Germans had made an unconditional surrender. The war was over! Ended! I don't remember the CO dismissing the formation. Men reacted every way imaginable. The celebration lasted a week! No close-order drills, no recruits to send to the front. German and French whiskey came from somewhere. We drank and laughed and drank some more. It had been a long, long war.

In reading my father's personal account, I wept and began to understand his need to crawl in a bottle. He had survived the carnage of major battles in World War II and became a decorated combat veteran, wounded not just physically, but mentally and emotionally from the trauma of war.

When the war in Europe ended in May of 1945, my dad returned home to the States and was stationed at Camp Campbell Tennessee with the 5th

Infantry Division.

With the scars of war, came mental and emotional anguish that did not have a course of treatment in the 1940's. Soldiers were expected to "be men" and swallow their pain, as any sign of weakness was intensely frowned upon. PTSD was yet to be defined or diagnosed, and counseling for such issues was far into the future. Because of this type of environment, many combat veterans turned to alcohol to numb the pain and quiet the nightmares— and my father was no different. He began drinking heavily when he returned from Europe, and this addiction would lead to his ultimate downfall, as others would use it to cripple him and break up his family.

A New Family

"Love is like war: easy to begin but very hard to stop."

H. L. Mencken

My father's world changed dramatically yet again when he married my mother in February of 1949, and chose to remain in the service. She was young and beautiful, turning heads everywhere she went. She had grown up poor as well, and looked forward to the stable lifestyle that the military provided, only I don't think she was quite prepared for the sacrifices required for such stability.

She was headstrong and very social, especially after being confined to the small town of Clarksville, Tennessee. She didn't drive, so was dependent upon my father to take her places—even the grocery store.

As is typical with Army life, my parents were transferred several times; including posts in the US, Japan and Europe, and the housing was not always spectacular. My mother had a penchant for nice things and needed a lot of attention, which was tough for my dad. As a Master Sergeant, he was often called away for training for long periods of time, leaving my mother home alone.

In 1951, my father would find himself back in combat once again during the Korean War. Fighting with the First Cavalry Division, this was a much different type of war than WWII—patrolling was difficult and bayonets seemed to jump out of the bushes and stab them in their backs. Preparation was the toughest. My father watched as thousands got themselves ready to fight by drinking sake, beating drums and tin cans, waving guns and sticks, and yelling at the top of their lungs. Suddenly, the opposition would be deathly quiet and then come running down the hillside. They had to cut them down as they came within range, and they just kept coming. They didn't dare allow them to overrun them, and though many brandished sticks, there weren't nearly enough weapons to go around.

Once the battle ended, thousands were dead. It was nothing like he had ever seen before. He was involved in two major battles like this before being sent to the rest area. For him, this marked the end of his combat years.

To further complicate matters, my father's drinking was showing no signs of abating, and often lead to serious arguments between my parents—my mother upset about his alcoholism and my father upset about her spending. They each had a crutch to deal with the lack of happiness in their lives that would cause a rift a mile wide between the two.

After the birth of us boys, Billy in 1952, Ricky in 1953, and myself in 1955, we found ourselves stationed in Orleans, France in 1957. The conditions there were not conducive to a stay at home mom raising 3 young boys, as we were all confined to one small room and no yard to speak of. Frustrations would often rise due to these claustrophobic conditions, and was a stress to my parents' marriage.

Following a bar room brawl (the first of several) that almost lead to my father being court marshaled, my family moved to Germany in 1958 via a hardship transfer with the Army. At that point, things weren't great by all accounts, but they were both trying to make it work. Upon arrival, my father was attached to the 3rd Armored Division and was met by his commanding officer, General Davis, whom he had served with in both WWII and Korea. He was obviously very concerned over the fact my father had put an American MP in the hospital.

"Bill, What the hell happened in Orleans?" General Davis asked sternly.

"Nothing really, sir," Bill replied.

"Nothing?! Damnit Bill you put three soldiers, one an American MP, in the hospital. You call that nothing??" barked General Davis.

"I've read the report and I understand the pressure you have been under, Bill, but we are not going to have that type of behavior here. Do you understand Sgt. Stanley?" he asked.

"Yes sir," Sgt. Stanley replied.

"Look Bill, I don't like some of these cocky young soldiers over here any more than you do, but you can't just go laying them out whenever one of them shoots their mouth off. You've got to ease up a little; lay off the booze a bit. It's getting to you," General Davis lectured.

"Yes, sir. Shit, General, now you sound just like Dee," Bill replied with a smile.

With a laugh, they stand to leave.

"Speaking of Dee, how is she?" General Davis inquired.

"She's good sir--same as ever."

"And the boys? I see you had two more."

"Yes Sir. Ricky and David"

"I read about David and his crippled leg in your file. I'm sorry to hear about that. There are great doctors here in Frankfurt though," said General Davis.

"I'm sure there are sir. I am sure he'll be fine," Sgt. Stanley replied confidently.

The General pats him on the back as he opens the office door for him.

"Walk with me Bill,"

"Look Bill, I mean it. I don't want to hear anymore of this nonsense—the bar fights or the drunkenness," warned General Davis.

"Yes Sir," Bill replied.

"By the way Sergeant, did you hear about the new recruit?"

A cadence of 60 men comes around the corner toward Bill and the General.

"New recruit?" Bill asked with a look of confusion.

General Davis turned towards a group of newly arrived soldiers, also attached to the 3rd Armored Division, marching by and pointed to 21-year-old Elvis Presley marching in line with the others.

"Seen our new arrival, Bill?"

"Oh shit, this place is gonna be mayhem," the Sergeant replied as he sees Elvis Presley for the first time.

A New Enemy

"I can't afford a whole new set of enemies."
Cecil Beaton

There was no combat action going on in Germany at that time. In the midst of the Cold War, Elvis Aaron Presley arrived due to being drafted by the US Army. The fifties was a time in American history where being in the military and serving one's country was something to be honored and respected, and Elvis was no exception. When his draft notice came, he willingly answered the call to serve.

He was a true patriot, and felt he should do his duty just like every other man in the country at that time. But Elvis wasn't exactly like the others and was allowed to live in his own home and travel with his entourage—including his father Vernon Presley, his grandmother Minnie Mae Presley, and two associates Red West and Lamar Fike.

It was a tough time for Elvis. His mother had recently passed away and he had sunk into a state of depression he would never fully recover from. The dichotomies of his life were stark—professionally he had never been bigger or more popular, yet personally he was overwhelmed with grief.

Gladys Presley and her only child, Elvis, were as close as a mother and son could be. She raised him to be a Southern gentleman with manners, respect, loyalty and compassion. His father was a bit of a rogue, and they were never really close. Gladys and Elvis were nearly inseparable until her death, and Elvis mourned her the rest of his life.

When Elvis arrived in Germany in 1958, the entire base became a bit star struck—especially the wives. Elvis was a phenomenon that is hard to describe or relate to in today's world. He was massive, epic, and unfailingly successful. Everything he touched turned to gold in an instant. Men and women alike worshipped him worldwide, and his willingness to serve only made him more likeable.

Though Elvis was a private person by nature, his father Vernon was not. Soon after his arrival, he was well ensconced at a local German club and that is where he first laid eyes on my mother—and she was a stunner. Clothed in a beautiful burgundy dress with pearls that set off her blonde hair and blue eyes to perfection, she was a sight to behold. In that moment, the course of history was forever altered and life as my father had known it would soon come to a crashing halt.

It was an evening like many others; the music was loud, the drinks flowing and the dancing lively. As my father twirled my mother around the dance floor, he couldn't help but notice all eyes were on her and he pulled her in closer.

As the song ended, my father and mother went back to their seats nearby, and the table was abuzz in talk of Elvis. Though my mother had never professed to be a diehard fan, she was still curious and wanted to meet him if she could. As her and my father chatted with their friends wondering who would get to meet him first, Vernon Presley made his way over to the table and introduced himself.

"Good evening, folks. I hope you don't mind my intrusion. I heard Southern accents from my table over there and it reminded me of home," Vernon explained.

"No, no intrusion at all," my father replied as he put out his hand.

"I'm Sgt. Bill Stanley."

The two shake hands.

"And this is my wife, Dee."

"A pleasure to meet you. I'm Vernon. Vernon Presley."

Both Dee and Bill are stunned speechless for a moment as they realize who is standing in front of them.

Bill recovers first, pulls a chair over for Vernon.

"Very nice to meet you, Mr. Presley. Won't you join us?" asked Sgt. Stanley.

"Don't mind if I do, thank you," Vernon smoothly replied.

Vernon sits between Dee and Bill and can't help but stare at Dee.

"So you're a little homesick, eh? Bill asked.

Vernon cracks a smile and chuckles as he says, "I couldn't be more homesick. Missing that fried chicken and grits like you wouldn't believe."

"Well, you're in the right place, my friend. My lovely wife here just so happens to put a scald on chicken you can't beat."

"Oh, Bill. I don't know about that. But you must join us for dinner one night, you and Elvis," Dee says excitedly.

Bill shoots Dee a stern look.

"I don't know about my son, but I'd be happy to come myself," Vernon said politely.

"I saw your boy this morning, Vernon. He looked really sharp out there with his platoon," Sgt. Stanley shared.

"Thank you Sergeant, that's high praise coming from you. Which division are you with?"

"I'm with the 51st ARB 3rd Armored Division," he answered.

"Good, good. How long you folks been over here?"

Dee pipes up, "We've been in Europe for months now, but only recently arrived here in Germany. We were transferred in from Orleans, France."

Vernon gazes longingly at Dee, drinking in her natural beauty and orders another round of drinks for the table.

"But you don't want to talk about the military, Mr. Presley," Sgt. Stanley said.

"Now Bill, let's not be so formal. Please call me Vernon."

"All right, Vernon. Where are you living while you're over here?"

"We're over at the Hotel Grunewald for now. Looking for a house though. The people who travel with us are a little cramped there."

Vernon shoots a look over at the bar, and Lamar Fike, one of the Presley bodyguards, signals Vernon with his index finger.

Bill follows his gaze, realizing for the first time that Vernon isn't here alone.

"Where's Elvis tonight? "Sgt. Stanley asked.

"He's home. He doesn't get out much at night," Vernon said.

"Must be nice," Bill replied.

Dee slaps Bill on the arm.

"Bill!" she exclaims a bit embarrassed.

"I'm just saying it must be nice. Hell, he's just a

private and he has his own housing."

Vernon gives Bill a concerned look.

"But he's not just any private Sgt. Stanley. There is no way he could live on base. He would attract too much attention and distract everyone from their duties," Vernon explained.

"That's right Bill," Dee agreed.

Vernon takes a sip off his drink and pushes away from the table.

"Well, folks, it's time for me to get on the road. It surely was a pleasure talking with you."

"Oh no, it's a shame you have to leave," Dee says dejectedly.

"Yes, Vernon, can't you stay a little longer? We'll order another round."

"Afraid not. I have to be getting along. But I tell you what, why don't we meet up tomorrow night and I'll buy us dinner. About seven--does that work for you two?" Vernon asked.

"That works fine, Vernon."

Bill stands and shakes Vernon's hand.

"Good, see you tomorrow then."

Vernon tips an imaginary hat to Dee.

"Ma'am."

"See you then, Vernon."

Bill and Dee watch Vernon move towards the door where Lamar is waiting. Dee is glowing from the encounter.

"Bill, I can't believe you said that to him earlier. I was so embarrassed," Dee says chastisingly.

Bill ignores Dee and continues to watch as Vernon and Lamer leave the club.

"He's a nice man. How about another drink Shotzie?"

The Forbidden Fruit

"In a time of universal deceit - telling the truth is a revolutionary act."
                                              George Orwell

The next day Dee was crowing to her neighbors and anyone who would listen about her meeting Vernon Presley the previous night. He was a handsome man, and oh so polite. She couldn't help but think he was quite the southern gentleman, and she noticed he couldn't take his eyes off of her the entire night.

She was a bit nervous about going to dinner with him. Dee was always self-conscious about her status in life and felt like she was in a race to keep up with the Jones'. And now she was having dinner with Elvis Presley's father—it didn't get much bigger than that. She spent most of the day struggling to decide what to wear. She hadn't had this much excitement in her life since...since never really.

As she scrambled to get dressed and get the boys ready for the baby-sitter, she hoped it would be a great night and that Bill wouldn't over do it. (Though if she were honest with herself, she wasn't opposed to tying one on now again either.) She so desperately needed something to look forward to, and befriending the Presley family fit the bill to a T.

"Boys!" Dee called out. You get your toys together--Mama's taking you next door to stay with Hazel."

"What about Betty, Mama? Billy asked. Why can't she come over and stay with us?"

"Betty has a date tonight, Billy," Dee replied. You love Betty's mother, Hazel, and she plays that candy game with you that you enjoy so much. Don't worry, we won't be home late."

"Hurray! I like Hazel. She plays Candyland with us," exclaimed Ricky.

The front door opens and Bill comes in, smelling of liquor, which wasn't unusual.

The three boys rush toward the door and salute their father.

He salutes back.

"How are my little soldiers tonight?"

"Good, Daddy," little David shouts happily.

He leans against his big brother Billy to steady himself as his leg braces are a bit awkward.

"Bill, Bill! Is that you? Hurry up, we'll be late," Dee says sternly as she rushes in from the bedroom.

She walks out to the living room, putting in her last earring and then stops as the unmistakable scent of liquor wafts over her.

"Gosh darn it, Bill. You've already had a drink, haven't you?' she asked accusingly.

Or two, more likely, she thinks to herself.

She turns and begins to gather the boys and ushers them next door to Hazel's. Dee couldn't help but think to herself that Bill's drinking was becoming a serious problem. She knew some things had happened to him during the war, but he never talked about it. Dee just couldn't understand why he didn't seem to be able to cut back when there were plenty of combat veterans who didn't drink in the middle of the day.

Dinner is over, and Dee, Bill and Vernon are drinking at their table while Lamar and Red West, another Presley bodyguard, watch from the bar.

"What do you think, Lamar? Red asked.

"I think they've had too much to drink."

Red nods his head in agreement and replies, "Yep. That's what I think too."

"Always trouble about now," Lamar said as they look towards the table.

"You've got a great sense of humor, my friend," Vernon says with a drunken laugh.

"So do you, Vernon. How 'bout another drink?" Bill slurs.

"Sure. Say, Bill, you won't mind if I have a dance with your lovely wife, will you?"

"Don't mind a bit. You two go right on ahead."

Vernon gives Dee a look and escorts her to the dance floor. They sway to Dean Martin as they begin to flirt a little.

"You're a mighty fine dancer, Dee," Vernon says with smile.

"Why, thank you, Vernon," Dee replies as her cheeks turn rosy.

As the two of them dance, Vernon pulls her closer.

Unbeknownst to them or Sgt. Stanley, a table of Air Force officers, obviously heavily drinking as well, are watching Dee and Vernon dance a bit too closely. Powered by liquid courage and the stupidity of ego, one of them walks over to Bill's table.

"You gonna let that Presley guy dance like that with your wife?" the officer asked a bit unsteady on his feet.

"Get the hell out of here, you punk. It's none of your damn business," Bill said with a look of warning.

"I'm just sayin', buddy. Those two are lookin' awfully cozy."

Suddenly, Bill rises and takes a swing at the goading officer, who promptly drops to the floor like a stone.

"What the hell?" he shouted as he rubbed his cheek.

By then, his four buddies are moving toward the table to jump in. One of them takes a swing at Bill, but Bill blocks the hit and gives him one in the nose. He falls instantly as blood gushes out of his nose.

Another officer in the group decides to give it a try himself and rushes Bill.

"You Army ass son of a bitch," he snarls as he launches himself at Bill. But Bill's too quick for him and dodges the blow.

Just then the club manager comes over just as

Red and Lamar reach Bill. They attempt to hold Bill back as the manager grabs the Air Force officer.

"All right, guys. Break it up," warns the club manager. "Let's take this outside. My customers don't need this kind of disruption."

By this time, everyone in the club is watching, including Dee and Vernon, slightly shocked at the turn of events. They follow the group outside where they're met by two MP's.

An MP turns to Bill. "What the hell happened here, Sergeant?"

"Nothing, just a slight misunderstanding," the Air Force officers interject.

"There is no misunderstanding, pal."

"These assholes were insulting my wife."

He lunges forward, but by this time, Red and

Lamar are holding onto him. Vernon inserts himself into the middle, and speaks politely to the MP's.

"Say fellas, how about we just forget this little incident and all go about our night," he suggests.

The MP's look around at the group.

"We're gonna let it go this time, but Sgt. Stanley, you better get on home," one of the MP's replied.

"Sure, why not?" Bill answers.

He shoots a dirty look to the Air Force boys as the walk back into the club.

"You two go on to the car. I'll get Dee's things," Vernon instructed.

"Thank you, Vernon. That's very sweet of you."

Vernon, Red and Lamer walk toward the club

and Vernon turns back toward them.

"Damnit Bill, you'd make a hell of a bodyguard, you know?"

Laughing, he and the boys go back into the club to gather Dee's shawl and handbag.

Back at home, Dee is livid that Bill embarrassed her, not only in front of the entire club, but Vernon Presley as well.

"What has gotten into you, Bill Stanley?" Dee asked with fire in her eyes.

"You just made us the laughing stock of the entire club, if not the entire base! How am I supposed to explain your behavior?"

"God damn it, Dee. If you weren't so busy being Vernon's lap dog, you would have noticed that people were starting to stare. I know he's Elvis' dad, but he's still just a person like you and me. You've got to cut it out with the hero worship. It's beneath you."

"How dare you! I was simply trying to be polite and friendly to him, especially after he was kind enough to buy us dinner. If you weren't such a brute, you wouldn't be in this mess. You're lucky the MP's didn't arrest you," Dee scolded.

"I'm sick and tired of you making excuses for your drinking and your temper. You're a master sergeant and a father for goodness sakes—start acting like it. You don't see General Davis or Vernon Presley acting like a fool and embarrassing their entire family," Dee snipped.

"I don't have to listen to this. I'm going to sleep."

Bill collapsed onto the bed in a heap and began snoring almost immediately.

Dee hung up her robe and crawled into bed

with a huff. She was pretty certain she had never been so mortified in her life, and wondered if Vernon Presley would ever speak to them again.

And So It Begins

"It's discouraging to think how many people are shocked by honesty and how few by deceit."

Noel Coward

The next day, Bill was up early and out the door to his post, preventing any further discussion. That afternoon, Dee invited a few of her girlfriends over to relay the events from the night before.

As they sit at Dee's kitchen table drinking coffee, Hazel and Arlene listen intently as Dee shares the disaster that was last evening.

"I tell you, girls, it was the most embarrassing thing you have ever seen in your life. Here we are, out with Vernon Presley, and Bill gets himself into a fight. A fight! I was so furious, I could have killed him," Dee fumed.

"What's Vernon like Dee?" Arlene asked.

"Vernon? Oh, he's very much a gentleman. If he hadn't sweet talked those MP's, Bill would be in the stockade right this very minute."

The phone rings and Dee gets up to answer it.

"Hello?"

"Good morning Dee. I hope I haven't interrupted you."

Dee immediately recognizes Vernon's voice. She points at the phone and mouths "Vernon" to Hazel and Arlene.

"No Vernon, not at all," Dee said sweetly.

"Dee, I just wanted to check on Bill. He drank

quite a bit last night and was a bit rowdy."

"That's very kind of you. He's just fine, thank you."

"Glad to hear it. Say, why don't the two of you come over to the hotel for lunch this afternoon?"

"Oh, Bill's still at work, Vernon."

"Then you come on over, Dee"

"My girlfriend is here with me and she drives. Do you mind if she comes along?"

"Not at all, I'll see ya'll in a little bit."

Dee hangs up the phone, smiling brightly. She quickly grabs her handbag and bids Arlene goodbye. Hazel reaches for her coat.

"Are you sure this is a good idea, Dee? Hazels asks hesitantly.

"Well, why ever wouldn't it be?" Dee replied astonishingly. "Vernon is just trying to make up for Bill's bad behavior and be a gentleman about the whole thing."

"If you say so," Hazel replied.

The ladies make their way to Hazel's car and pull out of the drive. Dee couldn't help but think that maybe last night hadn't been such a disaster after all.

Dee and Hazel sit with Vernon at a window table overlooking the quaint German street. Dee is an animated conversationalist and it helps to cover up Hazel's uncomfortableness.

"So Hazel, are you an Army wife like Dee here?" Vernon asks.

"I am Mr. Presley. I guess we've been an Army family ever since Max and I got married, about 20 something years now," Hazel proudly replied.

"And how do you find it?"

"How do I find it? I find it to be quite trying, especially when the boys are out on maneuvers for weeks at a time. Home alone with the kids, nowhere to go, nothing to do—it all gets very maddening at times."

Vernon nods in understanding.

"But I tell you, Mr. Presley, I wouldn't trade it for the world. Max is an Army man through and through. It's his life. And, to be fair, I knew all about it when we got married. So I can't complain—it was my choice."

"Good for you, Ms. Petersen. It seems like a hard life. And by the way, you can call me Vernon."

The waitress brings them more tea and clears the dishes.

"Can I get you ladies anything else?

Dee, more strudel?" Vernon asks.

"Good lord, no. It was delicious though. Thank you so much," Dee answers earnestly.

The two of them look at each other for just a moment too long, and the gaze isn't lost on Hazel.

"Oh my, Dee, look at the time. It's late and we need to get back." She turns to Vernon, "Thank you so much for the invitation. It was so very nice to meet you."

Vernon rises and pulls back Dee's chair and Hazel gets up on her own.

"The pleasure is all mine, ladies. Do come again, won't you? It's just me now, and I get bored with nothing much to do as well."

The women say their good-byes and walk through the beautiful archway to the hotel lobby, passing Lamar going the other direction. He does a double take at the women, and then sits down with Vernon.

"Wasn't that the gal you danced with last night that caused such a ruckus?"

"So?" Vernon asks gruffly.

Lamar puts his palms up in front of him.

"Just asking, Vernon, that's all."

A moment later, Elvis comes in and sits down at their table.

"Hi ya, Daddy. What are you two talking about?" he asks as he reaches for a piece of strudel.

"Nothing, boy. Nothing," he replied as Lamar gave him a knowing look.

As the ladies make their way home, Hazel can't help but wonder what was really going on. The undercurrent was obvious to anyone within 100 feet of those two, and she was afraid it would lead to nothing but trouble for her best friend.

"Dee darlin', are you sure you know what you're doing?"

"What in heaven's name are you blabbering about, Hazel? Vernon Presley is nothing but a new friend and a kind gentleman who's just as bored and social as we are. This is a whole different world over here for him too. And don't forget his wife just died and I'm happily married," Dee said emphatically.

"He has a crush on you, Dee. It's plain as day!"

"Oh don't be silly—that's hogwash. Can't a man and a woman simply be friends without everyone going into a tizzy?"

"I didn't mean to upset you, Dee. You're my best friend and I worry about you. Just be careful,

OK? You're a beautiful woman and he's grieving—that's a lethal combination," Hazel said with concern.

"Everything is just fine—I promise. Don't you worry about a thing," Dee replied reassuringly as she opened the car door.

Dee goes inside and hears the boys playing in their room. The sitter, Mrs. Becht, is gathering her coat, ready to leave.

"Thank you for staying, Mrs. Becht."

"Guten abend," she replies.

Dee hears ice cubes clinking in a glass and goes to the kitchen.

"Bill, what are you doing home?"

"It's almost 5:30, Dee. I come home every night at five o'clock. You know this."

"Unless you're out drinking," she says under her breath. "I didn't realize it was so late."

"Where have you been? The boys are hungry, there's no dinner and you're no where to be found."

Dee interrupts, "Bill, yes there is. Mrs. Becht made a dish for us, and it's in the oven keeping warm."

"Fine, but that still doesn't answer the question of where the hell you've been all afternoon," Bill said with an accusing stare and he took another sip of his drink.

"Hon, Vernon called and asked us to lunch--you and me both. Since you were working and not here, Hazel went with me."

"How come you didn't call me and see if I was free to leave?"

"Oh Bill, you know you couldn't have gotten

away. You're always complaining when you have to take time off. Besides, we'll see Vernon again I'm sure. You two seem to have really hit it off," she soothed.

"Still, you could have called and told me. And how is it the three of you had so-called lunch until 5:30 in the afternoon?"

"I suppose time just got away from us," she answered as she pulled dinner out of the oven. "Would you like another drink, hon?"

"Yes. Thank you."

As much as she hated his drinking, it was the only thing Dee could think of to distract him. He was so unreasonable when he was a few drinks in, and she didn't want him losing his temper around the boys.

"So, how was Vernon?" Bill asked.

"He's just fine it seems. He said to give you his

best and then mentioned something about you being a bodyguard."

"He did? What did he say exactly?"

"I don't remember, Bill. Why don't you just call him?"

"I'm not going to call him and ask him about it. Besides, we don't have his phone number."

"Sure we do, it's right here," she replied as she pulls a folded piece of paper from her pocketbook and hands it to him.

He takes it reluctantly.

"Sweetheart, why don't you go in and put the boys to bed while I set the table. They love it when you do story time with them. Mrs. Becht gave them their dinner and made sure they had a bath earlier."

"Alright then," Bill replied as he headed

upstairs. As he walked down the hallway towards the boys' bedrooms, he couldn't help but wonder if he was missing something, but quickly shook off the feeling. Dee loved him and the boys and was just excited to have a new friend—and being Elvis Presley's father didn't hurt.

A Seed of Doubt

"Any truth is better than indefinite doubt."
Arthur Conan Doyle

The next evening Bill and the boys roughhouse around the bedroom while Dee cooks in the kitchen. The doorbell rings, and Bill goes to the front door and opens it. He greets Vernon, along with his entourage, Red and Lamer, warmly.

"Hello Vernon, welcome. So glad you boys could make it. Come on in."

"Thank you, Bill. And this is for you."

Vernon hands him an obviously expensive bottle of whiskey.

"Why, thank you Vernon. You're too kind," Bill

said sincerely.

"And you remember the boys, Red and Lamar."

Bill nods and they all shake hands.

Dee comes in from the kitchen, wiping her hands on a dressy, frilly half apron she wears over her aqua dress. She has on the same fake pearls she always wears when she dresses up, and looks radiant as usual. This particular shade of blue really sets off her porcelain skin.

"Hello, Vernon. Won't you all come in?"

She nods at Red and Lamar.

"Make yourselves at home. Bill, why don't you get the boys a drink?"

Bill opens the gift bottle and pours drinks for all as Dee goes to the boys' bedroom to check in on them.

"Listen boys, we have some special guests for dinner tonight, so I want you to be on your best behavior, all right?" she implored.

"Who is it? Who's here for dinner?" the boys ask in unison.

"Just some friends of Mama's and Daddy's. Now wash up for dinner and remember to use your manners."

Everyone is gathered around the tiny table, almost too small for the four big men to sit comfortably. Casual conversation ensues, with the three boys speaking only when spoken to just as their Daddy has taught them, and they even remembered to chew with their mouths closed—for the most part.

"Dee, this is the best fried chicken I've ever eaten," Vernon exclaimed.

"Yes, ma'am, it's delicious. And this gravy is

really good," Lamar added.

Red chimes in, "Yes ma'am, delicious!"

"I told you boys that Dee here fries the best damn chicken you'll ever have the pleasure of eating."

"Thanks, you all. I just wish Elvis could have come, too," Dee responded.

Vernon nods while chewing.

"Do you think he could come some other time? I sure bet he misses southern cooking like you boys do," she implored.

"Now, Dee, Vernon doesn't want to discuss Elvis. He's got enough with all the people asking him for autographs and talking to him about Elvis every place he goes. Everyone follows him around like puppy dogs."

"Aw, it's ok, Bill. But I do want you two to meet

my son. He's a good boy," he replied.

He turns to look at the three boys, wanting to change the subject of conversation.

"You boys sure are the quiet ones. Cat got your tongues?"

"No sir, we only speak when spoken to. It's the rule of the house—especially when there's company," Billy said proudly.

"That's "house rule", son. And please don't talk with your mouth full," Bill corrected.

"Sorry, Daddy," Billy said with his eyes cast downward.

"What kind of games do you boys like to play?" Vernon asked them.

"Army, sir!" Ricky replied excitingly.

"Yeah, Army!" David echoed.

"Not surprising. Chips off the old block here. You got yourself some handsome boys, Bill. You ought to be proud."

"They are that Vernon."

Ricky, fork full of food, holds it halfway to his mouth, but with his head turned toward Vernon, listening intently.

"Ricky! Are you feeding your ear, son? 'Cus it looks like that to all of us," Bill said teasingly.

There is laughter all around the table as Ricky puts the fork in his mouth and chews his food silently.

Sometime later, dinner is finished and Dee gets the boys bathed and ready to go down for the night. She tells Bill they're ready for their story and begins cleaning the kitchen as Bill heads upstairs.

Vernon sits at the kitchen table, talking with her as she washes dishes. A few minutes later Bill returns to find him still there and the two of laughing heartily.

"Vernon, how 'bout another drink?"

He swiftly pours two glasses, full.

"Cheers!" Vernon says as they clink glasses.

The two men leave Dee in the kitchen and bring the bottle to the living room, where they proceed to drink the whiskey bottle dry. From time to time, Lamar and Red peek in the front from their perch to see if they're slowing down any.

"You boys come in out of the cold, now. I mean it," Bill shouted.

Lamar and Red come inside and move to the now dining room table, and talk amongst themselves. Bill and Vernon continue to drink heavily until Bill finally passes out on the couch. Vernon silently makes his way to the kitchen where Dee has just finished cleaning up and stands directly behind her.

She turns, and jumps back a bit.

"Oh, Vernon, you startled me," she said breathily.

"Your husband is, uh, sleeping on the couch, so I thought I'd keep you company…maybe give you some help," he said as he looked around. "Looks like I'm a little late, though."

"Good lord Vernon, I didn't need any help. Besides, you're a guest here."

Dee takes off her apron, straightening her dress. The two stand next to each other, leaning against the counter. Vernon slowly gets his arm situated around Dee and leaves it there.

She doesn't object and they begin to chat.

Soon, though, Vernon slips his hand around her waist and she moves closer to him, looking into his bright blue eyes. Vernon makes a move to kiss her, but is interrupted.

"Oh, sorry Vernon," a surprised Lamar said as he came back in from smoking outside.

Lamar hightails it back outside with a feeling of dread in the pit of his stomach.

"I tell you, Red, this whole thing is trouble. Nothing good will come of this."

"Ain't nothin' we haven't seen before, Lamar."

"I don't know, this seems different somehow..."

"Elvis is gonna be furious if he finds this out.

Red and Lamar walked back inside to the living room and find Bill passed out and Vernon in a bad way. They struggled to get Vernon down the steps and into the Mercedes, as he's had too much to drink yet again.

Suddenly, two MP's drive up, and stop behind the Mercedes.

An MP gets out and looks at Lamar. "What's going on here?"

"Nothing, sir, just heading home," Lamar answered politely.

"Is this man drunk? It's pretty late for you to be out here making all this noise," the MP replied sternly.

"He's not feeling too well. We'll just get him into the car here and on home."

The MP blocks the car door.

"Not so fast. Just what do you boys think you're trying to prove here? Where is it you're coming from?"

Lamar, remembering that everyone knows Sgt. Stanley, tries to turn Vernon's face from the MP's.

"Sir, we're just coming from Sgt. Stanley's place." He motions with his head toward the house.

"Bill Stanley, Sergeant Bill Stanley," the MP asks suspiciously.

"Yes, sir. Sgt. Bill Stanley," Red chimes in.

"You friends of his?" the MP inquired.

"We are sir, yes sir."

"And just why should we believe you boys, standing out here, this one drunk as a skunk?"

"Sir, if you want we can go back on over and get Sgt. Stanley for you," Red offered.

Both MP's think about this for a moment.

"All right. If you're friends of Sgt. Stanley, get on out of here. But you go straight home with this one," as he nods his head towards Vernon.

Lamar and Red hold their breath, hoping the MP doesn't recognize him.

"Yes sir," they replied with relief.

"Good night, then."

The MP's hop back into the jeep and take off and Lamar and Red load Vernon into the Mercedes and drive away feeling as if they've barely dodged a bullet.

A Wolf in Sheep's Clothing

"We have to distrust each other. It is our only defense against betrayal."
                                                Tennessee Williams

Dee wakes up the next day with a smile as her still drunk husband snores with the sounds of an incoming freight train. She knew Vernon was pretty intoxicated last night too, but he had put his arm around her and would have kissed her if Lamar hadn't interrupted. Dee knew this was getting close to being inappropriate, but she'd been so lonely for so long and craved the attention of a man who wasn't buried in the bottom of a bottle. Didn't she deserve to be happy too?

A few weeks later, Hazel and Dee are grocery shopping together and chatting about the upcoming week.

Hazel turns to Dee; "I just hope Betty can cook a decent meal for her sister while I'm gone."

"Oh Hazel, don't worry. The girls are not going to starve with you away for two days. If worse comes to worse, they can come over to our house for dinner or I can send Mrs. Becht over there to whip something up," Dee said reassuringly.

"Really? Oh thank you, Dee. That means the world to me." She paused for a second and asked, "Say, how on earth are you going to get around with Bill and Max out on maneuvers and me gone at the same time?"

Dee looks away, picks up a can of peas and pretends to study the label.

"Oh, Vernon is going to drive us," she replied softly.

"Who? What did you say? Did you say Vernon? Vernon Presley?"

"Yes, Vernon."

"Well, well, well. And what's Bill going to say about that? I can't imagine he'll approve."

"Don't worry so much Hazel, it was his idea," Dee informed her. He called Vernon himself and asked him. Vernon said it would be a pleasure to help a friend out. It's really not a big deal."

"Uh huh, I see," Hazel replied unconvinced.

Dee leaves the peas on the shelf and they continue to stroll down the aisle.

"Hazel, really."

"You like Vernon, don't you Dee? I know it. From day one, when we went to the hotel to have lunch, I could see it in your eyes. You have a crush."

"Hazel, don't be silly. Vernon and Bill have become good friends and he's just trying to help out. I don't know, maybe because they're both southerners. It doesn't really matter. The point is, Bill asked Vernon to drive us and Vernon accepted. You're making a mountain out of a mole hill."

"And perhaps another lunch at the hotel?" Hazel inquired with a bit of sarcasm.

"No, they moved into a new house," Dee replied.

"Aha! You certainly know a lot about Bill's good friend," Hazel answered.

"Stop it Hazel. I think it is very nice that Vernon is helping us."

"Besides, I have no one to drive me and David to the doctor for his checkup, and I don't want us to miss it."

"He's driving you and David to Wiesbaden?" Hazel asks incredulously.

"Yes, tomorrow," Dee said matter of factly.

Hazel says nothing, but pursed her lips in thought. She didn't know if she should be concerned or amused...probably both.

The next evening after driving to Wiesbaden for David's checkup, Dee sits in the kitchen, talking on the phone. She's all gussied up in a new navy blue dress with a beaded jacket accented by the gold necklace Vernon bought for her just that day. She twirls it lovingly around her fingers as she coos into the phone.

Vernon is on the other end of the phone and is equally dressed up in a gray suit, and looks quite spiffy.

He talks tenderly into the phone as Elvis walks

into his bedroom. He listens for a moment and senses something not quite right.

"Hey Daddy, who are you talking to? Elvis interrupts.

Vernon covers the receiver and says, "Just a minute, son."

Vernon goes back to Dee, but Elvis won't let him be.

"Daddy, is it that woman again? I thought I told you to stay away from her?"

Vernon's eyes shoot daggers as he turns his back on him to get back to Dee.

"Dee, listen. Why don't you take a cab to the club and I'll meet you there, all right?"

He hangs up the phone and turns around to face Elvis. "Damn it, son, this is none of your business!"

Elvis gives him a fiery look and replies, "The hell it isn't. Mama hasn't been in the ground more'n a few months and you're out running around already."

Now Vernon is steaming mad.

"Son, let's play it this way. You live your life and I'll live mine, alright?"

He turns and walks out of the room, and Elvis yells after him, "You have no respect for anyone but yourself and you're the most selfish person I know. I can't believe you're behaving this way!"

When Vernon arrives at the club, Dee is already seated at a very private, cozy table. Vernon rushes in, apologizing. A coat check girl comes and takes his coat as he sits down.

Vernon takes her hand in his and says, "Dee, forgive me for being late. I had a little, uh, business to take care of for Elvis."

"Oh Vernon, it's all right. When do I get to meet Elvis anyway? I'm dying to, you know."

Vernon is staring off into space and mumbles, "Who doesn't?"

"Excuse me, Vernon? I'm afraid I didn't catch that."

"Oh, nothing, Dee, nothing. You'll meet him someday, just not right now. It's just not a good time."

"Oh," Dee said with a pout.

"It's just that, well, he thinks we're getting too close and he doesn't approve."

"Oh, is that all? You know, Vernon, Hazel says the same thing and I just think it is the most ridiculous thing I've ever heard."

Vernon slowly reaches across the table and takes both of her hands in his.

"Is it, Dee?"

"Vernon, what are you saying?"

"You know what I'm saying, Dee."

They sit in silence for a moment, staring into each other's eyes.

Hazel, alone with a group of army wives comes into the bar, which adjoins the restaurant, chatting and laughing, but Dee and Vernon are caught up in their own world—oblivious to what's going on around them. The ladies take a table towards the front and order drinks, and Hazel excuses herself to go to the restroom. The drinks arrive and the waitress goes back into the restaurant.

Returning from the restroom, Hazel remarks, "This is a lot nicer place than the NCO club! Even the restroom is elegant."

Hazel reaches for her drink, notices it's not what she ordered and looks around for the waitress who is nowhere to be found.

"Hazel, is something wrong?" asks Arlene.

"No, everything's fine, I just didn't order this martini. I'm going to the bar to get my rum and Coke."

Hazel walks to the bar and sits on a vacant stool waiting for her drink, and mindlessly looks around the restaurant. She almost turns back to the bar when she spots General Davis at a table. He is staring intently at something across the room. Hazel follows his gaze and sees Dee cozied up with Vernon Presley, hands intertwined.

"Ma'am, here's your rum and Coke. I'm very sorry your order was incorrect," the bartender said as she handed her the drink.

Hazel nodded absently and continued to stare, furrowing her brow.

"Ma'am?"

Hazel turns slowly around, shaking her head.

"That's quite all right. Thank you," Hazel replied.

She picked up the glass and took a good, long drink. She barely heard the conversation for the rest of the evening and found herself lost in thought. What in the world was she going to say to her husband about what she just saw?

A Snake in the Grass

"The best way to destroy an enemy is to make him a friend."
Abraham Lincoln

The phone is ringing as Bill gets up from the dining room table the next afternoon. He's working on putting a model M60 tank together and wipes the glue from his hands with a wet rag.

"Hello?"

"Bill?" Vernon asks surprisingly.

"Vernon. How are you buddy?"

"Uh, good, Bill, good. When did you get back from maneuvers?"

"I just got back last night. It was murder. Hope we weren't too hard on your boy."

Vernon chuckled as he said, "No, he doesn't want any special treatment. Just wants to be a good soldier."

"Hey Bill, could you do me a favor tomorrow night?"

"Sure, Vernon, just name it."

"I'm going over to Frankfurt to a club, to see a big show. You know how it is when I do that, people everywhere, asking for autographs and trying to get close to me, so I thought you might want to come along, and kind of protect me so to speak."

"I'd be happy to, Vernon, but where's Red and Lamar?"

"They'll be tied up," he lied. "How about I pick you up around 6:30?"

"Sure Vernon. See you then."

As Bill hangs up the phone, Billy, Ricky and David storm in the room.

"Can we see the tanks, Daddy?" David asked excitedly.

"Have you brushed your teeth yet?"

"All done, Daddy. We're ready for bed," Billy replied.

"Yeah, Daddy, can we watch you for just a little while?" Ricky asked.

Bill pulls David up onto his lap. "Of course you can, boys. Just remember not to touch anything."

He moves the tank, which is almost completely built, to the center of the table so all the boys can see.

"Who remembers this part?" Bill points to the

barrel of the tank.

"The barrel!" Billy exclaimed.

"That's right, very good Billy. Now, how about this part? Ricky, you remember?"

"I think it's the turret, Daddy," Ricky said.

"Yes it is! Very good, Ricky!" he said with pride in his voice. "Now look at this."

Bill removes the turret from the tank model, exposing the inside of the tank. He picks up three plastic figures of army men and one by one, places them inside the turret.

"All right. Now, this is where the driver sits. David, you remember that for next time, ok?"

"Okay, Daddy."

"And this is where the loader sits," as he puts

the man in place.

"And this is the tank commander; he sits here. What do you boys think about that?"

"That's neat Daddy," Ricky said.

"Yeah, really neat, Daddy!" David chimed.

He sets David on the floor.

"Ok, soldiers, time for lights out. You go on in and I'll be there in a minute to tuck you in."

The boys scramble toward the bedroom as Bill replaces the turret on the model.

The phone call from earlier was still weighing on his mind. Something wasn't adding up and he couldn't dismiss that nagging feeling at the back of his mind. His gut was telling him Vernon was up to something. He only hoped he could trust Dee to be loyal to her family and realize the Presley's were no different and no better than the Stanley's.

Bill and Vernon sit in Vernon's car in front of the Presley house. Bill is in the driver's seat, and both have had too much to drink—but Vernon much more. He and Bill are talking and Bill is trying to figure out how to get him inside before he passes out.

"Bill, you are a hell of a man."

"Can't thank you enough for helping me out," Vernon said slurring his words.

"Any time, Vernon. Now, how about we get you on up to the house."

As he moves to the passenger side of the car, the outside light comes on and Red and Lamar walk to the doorway.

"Need some help, Bill?" Lamar calls out.

"I could use a hand here," Bill answered.

Lamar and Red meet him and the three of them drag Vernon up the stairs to bed. As Bill is about to leave, Elvis appears. Lamar introduces them, clearly uncomfortable.

"Bill, this is Elvis. Elvis, say hello to Master Sgt. Bill Stanley."

"Pleased to meet you, sir."

"Nice to meet you Elvis," Bill answered.

"Are you enjoying your time over here?"

"I am sir."

Lamar interrupts.

"Have Vernon pick up the car tomorrow."

"Will do Bill, thanks."

Bill walks to the car and gets in. He suddenly

realizes he just met Elvis Presley—Dee will be so jealous!

Elvis and Vernon: A Battle of Wills

> *"The great danger for family life, in the midst of any society whose idols are pleasure, comfort and independence, lies in the fact that people close their hearts and become selfish."*
>
> **Pope John Paul II**

Vernon and Lamar sit at the dining room table having coffee the following morning. Vernon seems to have recovered and is relating some of the hilarity from last night to Lamar.

"I tell you, Lamar, those women were all over us. Bill, being so tall and strong—we coulda' had any one of 'em," he announced.

"Why didn't you?" Lamar asked curiously.

"Come on, man. You know I've got it bad for Dee."

Lamar is visibly upset by this comment.

"For Dee? Damn Vernon, you're messin' with fire and you know it. That woman is Sgt. Bill Stanley's wife. This could cause a huge scandal for all of us. What if the press gets wind of it? What are you thinkin'?"

At that moment, Elvis walks in and sits down.

"What's going on? What are ya'll talking about?"

Minnie Mae, Elvis' grandmother, silently appears to pour him coffee and set a plate in front of him.

Neither one says anything.

But Elvis isn't easily deterred. "Lamar, what are

you two talking about?"

Lamar looks at Vernon pointedly and says, "Elvis, you better ask your Daddy about that," he says as he leaves the table.

"Daddy? Is this about last night? About Bill Stanley?"

An uncomfortable silence ensued and all at once Elvis begins to put two and two together.

"Wait a minute, was that Sergeant Bill Stanley last night? Is that Sergeant Stanley's wife you've been seein'?" he asks incredulously.

Suddenly, Elvis is furious. He starts pacing back and forth in the room at a loss for words. He knew his Daddy was a cad, but this was an all time low—even for him.

"Son, it's none of your business. Now, sit down here and have some breakfast."

"Breakfast? Breakfast? You want me to eat breakfast when you're carrying on with another man's wife? And a Master Sergeant's wife at that?"

"You're all riled up son, calm down."

"I will not calm down! Damn it, Daddy, you have to nip this thing in the bud right now. Stop seeing that woman immediately."

"Look here, Elvis, I will do what I want, when I want, and there's not a damn thing you can do about it," he shouted angrily.

Elvis stepped within centimeters of Vernon's face, and said, "I'm warning you, Daddy."

"You're warning me? That's rich," he scoffed. "Why don't you take a good look at yourself, son. You have no room to talk running around with that girl barely half your age."

With that, Vernon stormed out leaving Elvis

distraught and fuming.

The next day as Hazel is busying herself in the kitchen, she realizes she can't hold it in any longer. She has to tell her husband, Max, what she saw at the club the other night and what's been going on with Dee and Vernon. She doesn't want to betray her best friend, but something had to be done.

Hazel walks into the living room and sits on the sofa opposite Max.

"I need to tell you something, Max," Hazel said while wringing her hands.

"Well then spit it out," Max replied without looking up from his newspaper.

"When you boys were out on maneuvers, I went out with some of the girls to a club," she stammered.

"We were in the bar having drinks and I saw

General Davis and I saw Dee."

"You saw Dee with General Davis?" Max asked confused.

"No, of course not. General Davis was there by himself. I saw Dee with Vernon and they were, um, holding hands. General Davis saw them too," Hazel said as she looked at the floor.

Max puts the paper down and gives her his full attention.

"This can't be leading anywhere worth going. Maybe they were just having dinner and maybe you imagined they were holding hands. Maybe it was nothing," he said hopefully.

"Max, I'm a woman. I know things you could never know and I know that I saw Dee and Vernon holding hands. They were staring at each other with that look."

"And what look is that?" Max asked her.

Hazel looks out the window and takes a long drag off her Newport menthol cigarette, hoping to calm her nerves and then blows the smoke out slowly.

"The look of love, Max."

"Well, shit," Max replied as he slapped the couch with his paper and stalked out of the room.

Corporal William J. Stanley – 1942

Sgt. William J. Stanley – 1945

MSgt. William J. Stanley (fourth from right) – 1953

MSgt. William J. Stanley (seated center bench) in Germany – 1958

Dad with Billy, Ricky and Me – 1956

The Stanley Family – 1956

Me, Billy and Ricky with Vernon – 1961

Dee and Vernon sharing wedding vows –
July 3, 1960

Dee Elliott – 1942

Dee and Vernon's wedding - July 3, 1960

Dee and Bill in Japan – 1952

Dee and Vernon in Germany – 1959

Our new family – 1960

Vernon and Dee at Graceland – 1960

DAVID E. STANLEY

Billy, Ricky and Me with Elvis – 1967

Elvis and Me – 1967

Elvis arrives in Germany – 1958

Me, speaking with a Veteran in Normandy France – 1994

Me at Omaha Beach, Normandy France – 2007

My Father's final resting place

Blinded by Fame

Rather than love, than money, than fame, give me truth.
                                    Henry David Thoreau

The following morning at dawn, Bill and Max are overseeing their platoons checking out equipment on the tanks, readying them for the next day.

"Seen Vernon lately Bill?"

"Matter of fact, yes. The other night he asked me to escort him to a show he wanted to see. He asked me to act as his bodyguard. Keep the fans off and all."

"I see," Max said slowly.

Bill notices Max's tone and turns to look at him.

"What the hell does that mean? What's going on here Max?"

As much as Max doesn't want to get into the middle of his friend's marriage, he feels he can't hide what he knows. He would want to know if Hazel was stepping out on him with another man.

"Bill, you know you and I are friends, good friends."

"Sure, Max. Are you upset with me about something?"

"I wish it was that simple, Bill, but the truth is, well, the truth is Hazel saw Dee and Vernon having dinner while we were away—just the two of them."

Bill doesn't react right away and just stares at Max with a blank look on his face.

"Bill? Did you hear what I just said?"

"I heard you, Max, but I already knew they were having dinner. I asked Vernon to drive Dee and David to the doctor and wherever else she needed to go while I was out on maneuvers. They were probably just getting something to eat after the boys went to bed. No big deal."

"But, Bill..."

"But nothing," Bill said cutting Max off. "No big deal," he says as he walks away.

Max stared after him and shook his head. Not that he blamed him, but Bill just didn't want to see what was right in front of him.

After dinner, Bill sat in the kitchen lost in thought while Dee was next door playing cards with the girls. He picked up the phone, and dialed.

"Hello?"

"Vernon?" Bill asked.

"No, this is Lamar."

"Lamar, this is Bill Stanley. I need to speak with Vernon if you don't mind."

"Sure Sergeant, I'll get him for you."

Lamar sets the phone down and walks back into the living room where Vernon and Elvis are talking.

"Vernon, Bill Stanley is on the phone. He wants to speak to you."

Elvis shoots Vernon a sharp look as Vernon steps out of the room to take the call. He picks up the phone.

"Hello Bill, how are you this evening?" Vernon asked pleasantly.

Bill picks up his drink and takes a long drink.

"Well, Vernon, I'm fine. How 'bout yourself?" he asked a bit nervously.

"Good, good." Vernon replied.

"I just wanted to thank you for driving Dee while we were out on maneuvers. That was very kind of you and she couldn't have done it without you."

"You're very welcome. It was my pleasure. How is little David, anyways? I sure hated to see him being poked and prodded by that doctor."

"He's all right. He's used to the doctors by now. He's been in and out the hospital since he was born," Bill replied.

"Good to know," Vernon said.

"Those braces bother his brother Billy, more than they do him," Bill added.

"Well, he's a fine young boy—they all are, Bill. You should be proud."

"They're everything to me, Vernon. I would rather be with them than anywhere else. Kind of breaks my heart to have to leave them like I do," he said as he drains his glass.

"Vernon, I need to ask you a personal question. Did you and Dee have dinner when I was away?"

"Dinner?"

"Yes, Vernon, dinner. Did you have a fancy dinner with my wife when I wasn't here?"

Bill is starting to get a little angry, thinking about what Max had told him.

"Oh, that. Sure, man. I was running Dee out on some errands for the boys and it got late, so we decided to get something to eat. Dee said Mrs. Becht would have fed the boys already, so we got a hamburger. What brings this up, Bill?"

"It's just that I was told by someone who saw you the other night that it seemed a bit inappropriate the way you two were sitting together."

"Listen to me Bill. We're friends. And in my world that makes you a target. People are going to be jealous of our friendship and try to get in between us."

"I am sorry it's that way, but that's the price of fame. Do you understand where I'm coming from?"

Bill sits thinking long and hard about what Vernon just said. He wants to believe his new buddy.

"I do Vernon, but I had to call and hear it from you personally. Honor is all we have as men and soldiers. There is nothing I won't do to protect my family."

"I respect your honor Bill, and your family. I

would never do anything to jeopardize that. You have to know that. You have to trust me."

"I, uh, of course I trust you."

"You know Bill, I was thinkin'. You did such a good job for me the other night, and it's obvious you can take care of yourself and, well, probably several others," he said with a laugh.

"When we all get out of Germany and back to the states, I would like you to consider coming to work for us."

Bill is stunned speechless by the offer.

"Look Bill, I can understand you want some time to think about this. Get back to what you were doing. I will call you in a couple of days and we can discuss this further. Have a nice evening with your family."

Vernon hangs up and Bill sits on the couch,

holding the phone. He can't believe his ears. Slowly, his mouth breaks into a wide grin and he sets the receiver into the cradle. Dee was never going to believe this!

The Tactics of War

Money cannot buy peace of mind. It cannot heal ruptured relationships, or build meaning into a life that has none.
Richard M. DeVos

Bill is looking for Max the next afternoon and finds him sitting at the bar having a drink.

"Max," he said as he pulls up a stool next to him.

"The usual, bartender, and one for my buddy here too."

"What's with the grin, Bill?" Max asked.

"I got offered a job, Max."

"A job? Don't you already have a job, Bill?"

"No, no, not for now. I mean for when I get out."

"You're leaving the Army?"

"Max, get ahold of yourself. Of course I'm not leaving the Army. I'm talking about the future, when you and I both leave the Army."

"And?" Max asked quizzically.

"Last night, Vernon offered me a job as one of Elvis's bodyguards."

Max is stunned. He just stares across the bar at Bill incredulously.

"Well, Bill, that sounds nice," he said finally.

"Nice? That's all you can say? I just got offered a job with the most famous singer in the country, probably the world, and all you can say is nice?"

Max's eyes narrowed as he said, "Let's keep in mind it's by the man who took your wife to dinner Bill."

Bill glared at Max, and took a deep breath to control his temper.

"Oh, that. I already talked to Vernon about that. They just got something to eat after he drove her on some errands cuz it was late. No big deal."

"Bill, listen. I'm your friend, your best friend. I'm just saying, keep your eyes open. You have a beautiful wife and he's the handsome father of Elvis Presley. That's not a good combination."

Bill flies out of the stool and leans over the bar, face to face with Max.

"What the hell are you talking about? I just told you, they got something to eat. Now why don't you mind your own fucking business," he said angrily as he turned and stormed out of the bar.

"Sure, Bill, I'll mind my own business while Vernon Presley minds yours," he shouted after him.

Bill was furious as he stomped towards his jeep. Max had some nerve trying to make his wife out to be a tart right under his own nose. And after all Vernon was doing for him and his family. Vernon was right—people get downright envious of anyone who's friends with them. Unbelievable!

Bill walked in the door of the house excited to tell Dee about his conversation with Vernon last night, but he fell asleep before she came home from her card game, and was out the door before she got up.

Upon arriving home later that day, he looks for Dee.

"Dee?" Bill called out. "Where are you?"

He walked down the hall towards the sound of voices and was confused by what he saw. Vernon, Dee and his 3 boys were laughing as the boys opened up what looked to be presents.

"What's going on, Dee?" Bill asked.

Dee turned to look at him.

"Oh hi, Bill. Look at all the great toys Vernon got for the boys!" she said excitedly. "Isn't that so nice of him?"

"Vernon, I think maybe you should leave now," Bill said evenly.

Vernon looks at Dee who looks away.

"Bill, let's at least have a drink first."

"Vernon was just being neighborly."

"No, Dee, Vernon is leaving now."

He picks up Vernon's coat from the sofa and goes to the front door and opens it.

"Certainly, Bill. I know you must want some alone time with your family."

Vernon takes his coat, walks outside and Bill closes the door firmly.

"Now what in the hell is going on here?" Bill asked her sharply. "Why am I coming home to MY house to find MY wife with Vernon Presley and MY boys?"

"Bill, don't you dare talk to me like that! Vernon is a friend to both of us and to this family and he was trying to be nice. You're being completely unreasonable," she shouted back, "and I won't stand for it."

Dee stomped out of the room glaring at Bill as she walked by him. The nerve of that man! Drinking all hours of the day and night, starting fights in bars, getting arrested—who was he to question her conduct?!

Bill sat down on the couch and put his head in his hands. He felt like he was playing a game where he didn't know all the rules, but the other side did. He knew things hadn't been perfect between him and Dee, but they were still a family. He had to figure out how to get things back on track.

He tossed and turned later that night as he dreamt fitfully. It was Belgium in 1944 and he was standing next to a jeep on a wet road leading to a war torn town.

A General is in the jeep going over maps of the region. U.S. Troops from battle are walking past when suddenly three German Hitler youth soldiers rush the jeep from the field off the road. Instinctively, he pulls his Thompson Machine Gun and unloads a hail of bullets into the approaching boys. The boys instantly fall to the ground dead. Bill walks over to the bodies and discovers that one the boys has a white cloth in his hand. In that moment, he realizes what he has done. He stands in disbelief as the realization washes over him.

He cries out in his sleep. Dee instinctively jerks awake at the sound and shakes Bill awake.

"Bill! Bill! Wake up!"

His eyes snap open at the sound of her voice.

"What's going on? You're yelling and covered in sweat. Are you having that nightmare again?" she asked concerned.

"I'm fine," Bill stammers as he gets up and goes to the dresser and pours himself a drink. "It's nothing."

Over breakfast several hours later, Dee relays to Hazel what had happened the night before.

"I know Bill's always had a thing for his whiskey, but it's really getting bad. He was all hot bothered when Vernon brought presents over for the boys and just plain rude to him for no good reason!" Dee exclaimed. "And then he woke up yellin' and carrying on in his sleep again. I just don't know what to do anymore."

"Well, Dee he's under a lot of stress at work and he hates being away from you and the boys. It was probably hard for him to come home and see Vernon there," Hazel offered. "Maybe try and cut him some slack."

"Whose side are you on anyways, Hazel?" Dee asked with a frown.

"Now Dee I'm not going to beat around the bush with you. The real problem is you and Vernon gallivanted around town together and flaunted those gifts he keeps buying you right under your husband's nose. Now that's downright shameful and you know it," Hazel said sternly.

"Well, I'll be!" Dee said in annoyance. "You are really blowing this all out of proportion, Hazel. These dramatics are a bit much, even for you."

"When this all blows up in your face, don't say I didn't warn you, Dee. You're playing a dangerous game."

"I'm not playing anything, Hazel, so you can simmer down and finish your coffee. I've had enough of this ridiculous conversation." Dee said with a huff.

The Army Draws the Line

"You can't put abandonment and alienation under arrest."

Carrie P. Meek

Bill is sitting at his desk going over paperwork when General Davis appears in the doorway and knocks.

He stands to attention and salutes.

"Good morning, General. What a pleasant surprise. Please, have a seat."

General Davis sits in the chair across the desk from Bill.

"How's everything going, Bill?"

"Good, sir. Real good. Just looking over the final reports before we take the men out again," Bill answered as he nodded his head.

"Actually, I meant personally. How's everything going personally, Bill?"

"Fine, General. Sir."

The General looks him straight in the eye.

"Come on, Bill cut the crap. I know you've been hitting the bottle pretty heavy lately. What's really going on?"

Bill squirms uncomfortably in his chair. He knows the General is his friend as well as commanding officer and trusts him to understand.

"Ah, well, General..." Bill said as takes a breath.

"I think Vernon Presley might be getting too close to my wife and family," he said with a look of consternation.

"Bill, have you been drinking again?"

"No, sir. No sir I most certainly haven't," he said with surprise.

"Are you sure this thing you just said isn't just you overreacting a bit?"

"Sir, I have not been drinking. I just have this feeling, that's all. Some things have gone on, private dinners and such with my family and Vernon and don't seem quite right."

"Bill, damn it, think about what you're saying, will you? This is a battle you can't win." General Davis looks directly into Bill's eyes, trying to say with his eyes what he can't say with his voice.

"Bill, you and me, we're friends. We go way back in the service together, right?"

Bill nods in agreement.

"See, you and me, we're career military, period. I mean, what the hell else could we ever do? Sell aluminum siding for a living? Deliver milk? Hell no, we could never do either of those things."

"The army, it's our home, Sergeant."

"Of course, sir."

"What I'm trying to get through your head is to think about what you're saying with this Presley thing. Elvis Presley is not only a teen idol; he's become the poster child for the fucking United States Army. And that's bigger than you and me, Bill, so much bigger."

General Davis stands up and turns to leave.

"All I'm saying is think about what I've said. Will you do that for me, Bill? For your friend?"

"Sure, General. I'll do that for you. I'll think

about it," Bill said with a nod.

"Ok, then. I'll see you later on."

Bill salutes him as he leaves the office, then sits back down in the chair, confused. Was he really imagining things that weren't there? Maybe those dreams were getting to him after all.

Later that evening after the boys were in bed, Bill went to the bedroom to find Dee getting ready for bed herself.

"Dee, can we talk for a minute. I want to apologize for my behavior yesterday," Bill said as he watched her brush her hair.

She stopped and turned to look at her husband.

"I know I was harsh with you, and said some things I regret. Can you forgive me?" he asked sincerely.

"Of course Bill. Vernon is trying to help. I really wish you would lay off the drink some. That only makes you more agitated," she replied.

"I know honey, I know. I promise to do better," he said as he leaned down to kiss her forehead.

Sitting at breakfast with Vernon later that week, Dee is picking at her food.

"Come, now Dee, what is it? You've been quiet all morning. Tell me what's bothering you," Vernon prodded.

"I'm worried, Vernon. Now that the men are back, I'm afraid Bill will find out how much time we've been spending together. I mean, it's one thing to go out while they're away, but now, I just don't know. It doesn't feel right," Dee said with a frown.

Vernon reaches across the table and takes her hand, holds it in both of his.

"Now hon, look. You don't have to worry your pretty little head about anything. I'll always take care of you, you know that," he said as he squeezes her hand.

"Dee, I will always be here for you. Nothing is going to happen."

Dee seems somewhat relieved and a slight shiver goes through her as Vernon leans closer.

"Vernon, I just don't think I can do this. I mean, I'm married and have a family. What if someone finds out? What about my children? I'd just die if I hurt them."

"Dee, do think about your children. I can give you and the boys a life that you could never have with Bill. That you could never have with anybody else. Think what that would mean to your sons - the best schools, the best clothes, the best home. What do you think Bill will be able to provide when he's kicked out of the army for drinking, fighting and disorderly conduct? Then what will you do? He's my friend too, but he's headed down a bad path and just won't change course. Dee, admit it. He's a damn drunk. He'd rather be hanging out in the NCO club with his war buddies than spending time at home with his family."

Dee thinks about what Vernon is saying and nods slowly.

"I do want the best for my boys, and I'm worried sick Bill is going to drink us into the poor house. But Vernon, it's all so sordid..."

"Is it, Dee?" he asked. "No one planned this. We couldn't help we met and fell in love and that Bill won't stop drinking. Things just happen sometimes."

"So you are in love with me?," Dee asks with a smile.

"You know I am, Dee. I have been since the first day I laid eyes on you," Vernon replied.

"I love you too Vernon, and I just hope you're right," Dee said shakily.

"I've got it all under control, my dear. You can trust me," Vernon replied.

A Wife Abandoned

*"Plant and your spouse plants with you;
weed and you weed alone."*
                                   Jean-Jacques Rousseau

Dee walks quickly up the steps and raps on Hazel's door. She's changed and is now wearing capri pants, black flats and a warm jacket. The garnet necklace hangs around her neck.

"Dee, what a surprise. I thought I saw you go out earlier," Hazel exclaimed.

"Are the girls home, Hazel?"

"No. They went to the library." She closes the door and walks into the living room with a look of concern.

"Dee, what's wrong? Has something happened? Where's Bill?"

"He went to Paris and was supposed to be home last night, but I haven't heard from him. Probably got drunk again knowing him."

Hazel sits on the couch next to Dee.

"What in the world is going on then?" Hazel asked.

"Oh Hazel, I'm so confused," Dee said with tears in her eyes.

She breaks down and starts to cry. Hazel comforts her as she pours her heart out about her conversation with Vernon and the problems she'd been having with Bill.

Dee jerks suddenly, perking her ears towards her house. She hears her phone ringing and runs to answer it.

"That's probably Bill now," she said to Hazel as she runs next door, into the living room and answers the phone.

Hazel follows behind her, arriving just as she answers.

"Hello? Bill?"

"Dee, is that you?" her sister asks.

"Oh, Peggy, it's you. How are you?"

"Dee, I'm afraid I have some bad news here. Daddy died this morning," her stepsister said sadly.

Dee drops the phone and bursts into tears for the second time. All of the day's happenings have done her in, and she's emotionally exhausted.

Hazel goes over and takes the phone from Dee, talks to Peggy and then sets the phone back in its cradle. She takes Dee in her arms and hugs her.

"Oh Dee, I am so sorry. What a terrible thing," Hazel said as she comforts a still crying Dee.

She pats Dee on the back as she sobs, and then leads her to the sofa.

"What can I do? Should I call anyone? What about Bill? He's not here, right. Where are the boys?"

Just as she was asking, the boys came running in the front door with Mrs. Becht, laughing and carrying on.

When they see their mother crying, they rush to her and climb up on the sofa.

"Mama, what's wrong? Billy asks worriedly as he pats her on the back.

"Boys, I'm afraid your grandfather died back in the States. Your mother is pretty sad right now. How about we let her catch her breath. You all come with me. We'll play Candyland and make grilled cheese sandwiches."

Hazel stands, gathers the boys and heads out the door.

"Mrs. Stanley, is there anything I can do?" Mrs. Becht asks.

"No, Mrs. Becht, thank you. You go on home now. We'll be ok."

"But where is Mr. Stanley?" she asks.

"He's, um, he's not here...as usual. Go on, I'll be fine."

Mrs. Becht leaves and Dee walks into the bathroom looking for tissues. The phone starts ringing once again.

"Bill? Is that you?" Dee asks with frustration.

"No, Dee, this is Vernon. Is everything all

right?"

"Oh, Vernon, Daddy died today and Bill is MIA," she sobbed.

She breaks down again, wiping her nose with a tissue.

"You stay put. I'll be right there," Vernon said as he raced out the door to his car.

Vernon pulls up to the Stanley house and walks inside. He sits on the sofa next to Dee and puts his arms around her, and hugs her as she cries.

"Vernon, we have to stop all this now. I've been thinking about it and I just can't do it. My family is everything to me. Now I've lost my Daddy so all I have left is Bill and the boys, and I have to think about what this would do to the boys."

Vernon nods understandingly and pulls her closer.

"Dee, where is Bill? I know they're not on maneuvers, why isn't he here with you?"

She raises her head and looks at him a bit unsure of herself as she struggles to decide what to do.

"I don't know. He was supposed to come home last night from Paris, but he never showed."

"Dee, you listen to me. I'm here now. We're going to make everything all right again for you. Now, what do we need to do? Would you like to go back for the funeral? Take the boys with you?"

Dee is thinking again as a single tear runs down her face. This one isn't for her Daddy.

"I'm not sure, Vernon. I'm so confused."

"Listen, hon. We can go back to the States right now, you hear? I can make a call and we can be on the next plane outta here."

"I don't think so, I don't think we can make it in time. Peggy said the funeral is the day after tomorrow."

"All right. Do we need to send flowers or anything to Peggy? Does she need money for the funeral?"

Dee looks up at Vernon as he wipes the tear from her eyes.

"Whatever you need, Dee. Whatever you need."

He wraps her into his arms just as Bill walks into the house, stumbling slightly and obviously drunk. He sees the two of them and instantly became angry.

"What the hell is going on here?" he shouted.

"Her Daddy died, Bill. She's pretty upset," Vernon said sharply.

Dee wipes her eyes and looks at Bill.

"Daddy's dead, Bill. Vernon's just trying to help me figure out what to do since you weren't here and no one knew how to find you," Dee replied accusingly.

"I can see that," Bill said sarcastically.

He moves from the doorway and tries to sit in the chair, but stumbles and falls down awkwardly into the cushion.

"Where have you been anyhow?" she said with annoyance. "You were supposed to be back last night from Paris and you never showed and never called."

"A first sergeant asked me to go to Paris with him, so I did. But then he left me there. Well, he didn't actually leave me because he's still there. But I had to get someone from the unit to come over and get me...."

Vernon jumps in suddenly, "Bill, let's stop the

bullshit, shall we? Dee needed you and you weren't here because you were too busy drinking with your buddies as usual."

Bill jumps out of his chair, picks up the lamp on the table and throws it across the room hitting the wall with a loud crash. The lamp breaks into a thousand pieces as glass goes everywhere.

"God damn it, Vernon, don't even think about insulting me in my own home. Dee's my wife—not yours and it's time you start remembering that," he yelled as he fell back into the chair.

"Now I think you should leave Dee and I alone. You're not welcome here anymore."

Vernon picks up his coat and opens the front door and turns back.

"Call me, Dee, if you need anything."

She gives him a grateful glance, and then looks

over at Bill who is about to pass out in the chair.

"Bill, Bill, can you hear me?"

Bill rouses himself and looks at Dee with bleary eyes. "Sure, hon, I hear you. And I'm sorry about your Daddy dyin' and all."

"Bill, we need to talk. We need to talk right now. Our family is falling apart because of your drinking and I can't take it anymore."

"Let's talk tomorrow, all right."

He blacks out in the chair.

"Sure, Bill. We can talk about it tomorrow," she replied wearily as tears begin rolling down her cheeks. She stares out the window wondering where everything went wrong and how she got to such a place.

Vernon Under Fire

"Without a family, man, alone in the world, trembles with the cold."
Andre Maurois

Lamar and Red sit at the kitchen table playing cards back at Vernon and Elvis' place. A pretty, dark haired young girl, Priscilla Beaulieu, is on the sofa and Elvis is at the piano playing a gospel song. Muffled noises are coming from the other room, and Elvis looks up from the piano with an annoyed look on his face.

"Oh, Vernon," Dee says with a giggle as she sits on the bed in Vernon's room.

Elvis slams his hands down on the keys of the piano in frustration.

"Careful, there E. You don't want to break that thing," Lamar scolded gently.

"Lamar, this has to stop."

"I know, I know. That Bill Stanley is a big son of a bitch and he might just beat the hell outta Vernon if he's not careful."

Suddenly, Vernon and Dee appear in the doorway, laughing and holding hands.

"Daddy, I need to talk to you," Elvis said sternly.

"Sure, son, but first I'm going to take Dee home."

"Let Lamar do that, this is important," Elvis replied.

Vernon shrugs and kisses Dee goodbye.

Red signals to Priscilla still at the piano and the two of them walk out of the room.

"What's so dog-gone important that I can't even drive Dee home?" Vernon asked with frustration.

Elvis starts to pace around the room as Vernon sits down on the sofa with a huff.

"What's so important?" Elvis asked incredulously.

"Yes, Elvis, what's so important?" Vernon repeated.

"God damn it, Daddy, this thing with this woman is gettin' out of hand."

"She has a name son. Her name is Dee."

"Yes it is, Dee Stanley. Wife of Sergeant Bill Stanley, the same Bill Stanley I'm serving with in the

United States Army right here in Germany. What if this gets out? What if my manager, Colonel Parker finds out?"

"Don't disrespect me, son. What's your damn point?"

"My point is, what the hell are you doing with her? There's all kinds of women over here who are single and wouldn't cause a lick of trouble--go sleep with one of them."

"There are, huh? And what about you, son? I see you're still courting that 14-year-old? What do you have to say about that?"

"God damn it, that's none of your fucking business!" Elvis shouted as he continued to pace back and forth.

"This is not about me, Daddy, this is about you. This nonsense could cause a scandal that could get me kicked out of the Army and ruin my career!"

"Don't worry, son. I've got it all under control. There won't be a scandal—I promise you.

Elvis turned and walked out of the room in frustration and said under his breath, "I just bet you do..."

A Persistent Enemy

"The great enemy of the truth is very often not the lie, deliberate, contrived and dishonest, but the myth, persistent, persuasive and unrealistic."

John F. Kennedy

Later that night, Bill and Vernon are sitting at a corner table. They've had several drinks already and order another.

"Listen, pal, I'm sorry about what happened at your house last week. Dee was just upset about her Daddy dyin' and she was worried when she couldn't find you. I didn't mean to overstep my bounds, Bill. I was just trying to help you and Dee through a bad situation," Vernon said as he shook the ice in his glass.

"Forget it Vernon, I'm just a little worried about

things at the base, that's all. It's got nothin' to do with you. I know you were just trying to help."

"Well, Bill, you sure don't have to worry about your family. You are a very lucky man. Dee is a wonderful woman and I wouldn't dream of interfering with you and your boys." Vernon signals the waiter for another round as he changes the subject.

"Bill, I was just thinking about how much you like the Mercedes I've been drivin' around. I'd like for you to have it when I leave Germany as a token of my friendship."

The waiter sets down the drinks in front of Bill and Vernon. Vernon holds up his glass and Bill follows.

"To our friendship," Vernon announced.

"Sure Vernon... to our friendship," Bill said after him.

They clink their glasses together and Bill takes a

big gulp from his drink while Vernon puts his down, untouched, and watches Bill spiral down the familiar hole of drunkenness.

After yet another long night of drinking, Bill walks in to Max's office just as he's getting off the phone.

"Damn Bill. You don't look so good. Have a seat. What the hell happened to you?"

"I fucked up, Max. I fucked up big time. I got arrested and will probably be relieved of my duties as Master Sergeant, effective immediately."

"Christ, Bill, how in the world did that happen?"

"I drank all night with Vernon, and didn't stop until sunup."

Well, you look like you're still goin' there buddy," Max observed.

Bill looked down at the floor as his cheeks burned with shame.

"Ah, that's what they got you for, didn't they? Being under the influence while on duty. Damn it, Bill, what were you thinking?"

"What you told me, before. Vernon trying to take them, Max. I just know it."

"Take your family? Max asked.

"Yep," Bill replied dejectedly.

"Shit, Bill, don't let him. My god, fight for them. There's got to be a better way than this. You're just feedin' right into his hands."

"What can I do? It hurts, Max, hurts bad. I love Dee but how can I compete with the Presley's? What his dad wants, he gets. And I think Dee wants it too. And if she didn't before, she will now once she finds out I'm in trouble again. I'm going to lose my boys,

Max," Bill said with desperation in his voice.

"Drinking all night isn't going to help, Bill. You know that. You gotta get it together, man. Get off the booze. Don't let this thing ruin your career and your family."

"I don't know what to do. The booze is the only thing that kills the pain."

"Why don't you tell someone about this? Don't let Vernon get away with what he's doing. You can't just sit around and drink yourself into the bottom of every bottle you can get your hands on. They'll use it against you."

"Tell someone?" Bill asked with a mean laugh. "Right. And who would I tell, Max? My commanding officer? General Davis? Smith? Who?"

"Why not General Davis? You two go way back; he's bound to believe you and want to help. He saw

Vernon and Dee having dinner at the club that night."

"Listen Max, I may be two sheets to the wind right now but I do know this - I can't fight the Army because of the publicity with Elvis. You really think they're gonna allow that to happen? And I can't fight Vernon because of the Presley fame and fortune. I've talked to Davis and he said nothing, looked at me like I was crazy and shook his head. So you tell me, Max, what can I do?" Bill cried out as breaks down in tears. "What the fuck can I do?"

Max watched Bill leave his office with his shoulders slumped and he couldn't just stand by and watch his friend lose his career and his family. The next day as Max walked down the hallway he runs into General Davis.

"Pardon me General, can I have a word with you?"

"Of course. What can I do for you?"

"I want to talk to you about Bill Stanley. He's in a bad way."

"Now I'll stop you right there as I know he's your friend. Bill's been restricted to his quarters as of this morning and that's where he's going to stay for a while. He's been relieved of duty and there's going to be a hearing if he keeps this up."

"Keeps up the drinking?" Max asked.

"No, keeps on telling this convoluted story about Vernon Presley stealing his family right out from under him."

Max looks sharply into the General's eyes, waiting for him to acknowledge he knows the truth of that.

The General turns to leave, then turns back. "Tell him, Sergeant, tell him to stop it right now. I can't protect him any longer. I've done all I can."

The General turns and walks away as Max watches him disappear down the hallway. Max couldn't help but think he'd done all he could for him too.

Vernon Prevails

"In war, whichever side may call itself the victor, there are no winners, but all are losers."

Neville Chamberlain

Vernon and Dee sit on Dee's couch together talking earnestly about the future. With Bill demoted, his pay cut and all of them publicly humiliated, Dee is at her wits end. She just can't take it anymore. She has 3 boys to think about, and no way to take care of them by herself.

Bill's drinking had reached the breaking point, with no signs of abating. She was going to have to make some tough decisions in order to protect her boys.

Bill is following an MP outside the barracks

towards a car that he recognizes as Vernon's Mercedes. His heart starts racing as he nervously wonders what he's doing here.

Vernon walks up to him and the MP says to the both of them, "You have five minutes."

He posts himself near the car as he sees Dee exit the passenger side.

"Dee, what the hell is going on here?"

"I've made plans to go back to the States, Bill. And I'm taking the boys. You are no longer fit to be a husband or a father and I can't sit idly by and watch you destroy this family any longer."

"Where will you be?" he asked suspiciously as he eyed Vernon.

"Peggy's place," Dee said firmly.

"Peggy's place?" Bill asked incredulously. "Why

she lives in a trailer, there isn't room for you all there. That's not realistic, Dee."

"Regardless, that's where we'll be."

"Why are you going, Dee? Please tell me. Is it Vernon?"

"No Bill, its you. I'm tired of living here, tired of being a military wife to someone who cares more about drinking than he cares about his own family. I want a house with a yard and trees and a place where the boys can play. A town where they can make friends and not have to move every year and wonder if their dad will be home to play with them or if he'll be too drunk yet again."

"Now look here, Dee. You knew when you married me the kind of life we'd have. Why was it ok then and not now?" Bill looks past Dee and into the car. Vernon sits at the wheel, looking straight ahead.

He looks dejectedly at Dee as said "I suppose there's nothing I can do about it now, is there? I'm not exactly in a position to fight you on this."

He looks at her pointedly and she finally looks up at him--the man she once loved.

"There's going to be a hearing this afternoon, but I want to say good-by to the boys first."

Dee's eyes well up with tears as she shakes her head in disappointment, but she doesn't stop herself from walking away. She gets into the car and she and Vernon drive away.

Bill watches the car fade into the distance and the MP leads him back to his barracks. He had a feeling he had just lost everything.

That afternoon, he was found guilty of being intoxicated while on duty, demoted to the rank of Sergeant First Class from Master Sergeant, and fined

$100.00. His life as he knew it was officially over.

As Bill walked back to his house following the hearing, he puts out his cigarette and decides to stop next door. He knocks and Max answers, steps outside and quickly shuts the door.

"Damn, it's cold out here."

"Let's go inside then," Bill replied.

"Can't do it, Bill. Hazel doesn't want anything more to do with this whole thing," he said. "It's really upsetting her."

The two stand on the porch in silence, lighting up two cigarettes.

"I heard about the hearing, Bill."

"Yep, I'm a First Sergeant now," Bill said dejectedly.

"I'm real sorry, Bill, real sorry."

"My own fault, I guess. I've got no one to blame but myself."

"Maybe you should just let Dee go, Bill. You're in no condition to care for your family right now. Maybe Vernon and the Presley's are what's best at this point."

"But she loves me, Max, I know it," Bill said earnestly.

"No she doesn't, Bill. No she doesn't. Your marriage was over right about the time you didn't show back up from Paris when her Daddy died. That was the straw that broke the camel's back. It was only a matter of time until she left you. The drinking while on duty and demotion were the nails in the coffin. You did this to yourself, Bill"

A few days later they are all gathered at the

airport in Frankfurt. The day is dark and it's lightly raining. Dee and the boys are dressed up and carrying small bags, as Vernon is trying to cover them with a large umbrella.

Bill starts to tell them good-bye with tears in his eyes. He hugs Billy first.

"Good-by, little soldier. Now remember, you take care of your little brothers for me. I need you to be strong."

"I will, Daddy. But when are you coming?" Billy asked a bit confused.

"Soon, Billy, I promise."

Bill turns to hug Ricky, then David. All three boys salute him and he salutes back.

Suddenly, little David runs over to Bill and hugs his leg. Bill picks him up and David hugs his neck tightly.

"Bye, Daddy. I love you," David said as Bill set him back down.

Tears well up in Bill's eyes again as the four of them board the plane. He makes his way back and out of the airport with Vernon trailing behind. They get in the Mercedes and drive off towards a bar not too far from the Army base.

Vernon and Bill pull in the parking lot and walk inside. They sit down without talking to each other as Bill smokes one after another. A bottle of whiskey sits beside his glass and he keeps refilling it as fast as he can possibly down them.

Bill turns to Vernon and says, "You're behind this, aren't you? You put this idea into Dee's head and now she's gone."

Vernon looks at him sternly and says, "I am Bill, I am. It's what's best for Dee and your boys. You're in no condition to be a father or a husband right now.

You should take the opportunity to pull yourself together."

"But why, why are you doing this to me? A man needs his family, Vernon."

"It's for the best, Bill. It's time you accepted that and moved on."

"So there is no job, no car, no nothing is there. It was just a fucking lie all this time in order to keep me from seeing what was going on right under my nose."

"That's right Bill. I did what I had to do to help Dee and the boys."

"But she loves me Vernon. We're a family."

"No, Bill, she loves me now and I love her. Your drinking and fighting killed the love she used to have for you and it's not coming back."

"I'm doing the right thing here, Bill. You should know that. Dee and the boys are better off with me, and it's high time you come to realize that. There's not a damn thing you can do about it anyways," Vernon said angrily.

He slams his empty glass down on the bar as the bartender comes by and pours another drink for Bill. Bill starts to take a drink.

"Yeah, Bill—have another drink. That's what you do best anyhow."

Bill leaps off the stool and throws Vernon up against the wall.

I'll kill you... you lying son of a bitch. You're not going to get away with this!" he shouted.

Three MP's rush Bill and pull him off Vernon. They escort Bill out of the bar as Bill continues yelling at Vernon.

Vernon fixes his ruffled coat, pulls cash out of his pocket and pays for the drinks.

"You all right there buddy," the bartender asked Vernon.

"I'm fine. Just fine." He turns and walks out of the bar.

The Ultimate Betrayal

"The victor will never be asked if he told the truth."

Adolf Hitler

Bill's behavior in the bar with Vernon makes its way back to General Davis. It's left him no choice—Bill has to be quieted before the whole damn thing blows up on all of them. He feels sorry for him, but his hands are tied. He picks up the phone and makes a call.

Sometime later, Bill wakes from a drowsy sleep. A white-coated doctor with black glasses stands next to his bed and writes on what appears to be a medical chart.

"Where am I?" Bill asked slowly.

"You're in the hospital, First Sergeant," the psychiatrist replied.

"But what am I doing here? Am I sick?" he asked with confusion.

"You were brought here by the MP's. Seems you were mumbling some crazy story about the Presley's stealing your family."

"It's Vernon. Just Vernon."

"What?"

"It's Vernon Presley, not Elvis," Bill replied.

The doctor snaps the clipboard and looks at Bill.

"Same difference. Anyway, I believe you mentioned something about taking his life or your life; it was slurred from all the whiskey you'd been drinking. I did speak to your regimental commanding officer, General Davis, and he said that to his knowledge, you had no intimate involvement with the Presley family."

"That's a damn lie," Bill shouted. "He knows full well what's been going on. He saw it with his own eyes at the club, and I talked to him about it myself. Get him on the phone, he'll tell you I'm not lyin'!"

"Look, First Sergeant, you're in a lot of trouble from what I understand, so it might be the best thing to just keep your ramblings to yourself."

"If you don't believe me, I'll call Vernon Presley and tell him to come over here right now. He'll confirm everything I'm telling you."

The doctor walks to the door.

"Sure, you go ahead. The phone is in the lobby."

Bill sits in a vinyl chair near the front door of

the hospital. He's still wearing a hospital gown, but has put his jacket on over it. Suddenly he sees Vernon enter the front door wearing a cashmere coat.

"Vernon, you gotta help."

Vernon looks at him cautiously.

"Bill, what kind of trouble are you in now?' he asks as they walk inside and down the hallway.

"I just need you to tell this doctor you know me. Please. Tell him what's happening. Tell him what you doing to me and my family."

Bill stops at a door with a huge window in the top and knocks loudly.

The psychiatrist looks up, hangs up the phone, and opens to the door.

"Doc, this is Vernon Presley."

"Mr. Presley, thank you for coming over. We do really appreciate you taking time out of your day. I know you're a busy man," the doctor replied as they shook hands.

"Thank you, First Sergeant, I'll take it from here."

He leads Vernon into the office and closes the door. Bill waits in the hallway and smokes another cigarette. He watches the two talking through the window and wishes he could hear what they're saying. He sees the doctor pick up the phone and dials.

"Yes, sir, Mr. Presley is here with me now," the doctor says into the phone. He says he has met Bill Stanley on occasion as they're drinking buddies, but has no idea what the rest is all about.

"What do you want me to do, sir?" the doctor asked.

The psychiatrist pushes a button on his phone as Vernon looks on.

Suddenly, six orderlies come running into the hallway and drag Bill into a tiny windowed room and lock the door. He pounds on the door with his fists, and then goes to the window that looks out into the hallway.

He sees Vernon shaking hands with the doctor.

As he watches Vernon, three orderlies come back with a needle and a straight jacket. He tries to escape their grasp, but they get the shot into his arm despite his best efforts. As they struggle to get the straight jacket on, Bill starts screaming at the top of his lungs.

"Nooooooooooo. Look at him, he's taking my wife, he's taking my boys, he's stealing my family! You've got to believe me!"

At his final scream, he sees Vernon calmly walk down the hallway, coat over his arm. He tries to grasp the glass and as he slides down to the floor. Vernon exits the hospital without looking back.

Later that day Bill is lying inside a military transport plane wearing a straight jacket, and awaiting transfer back to the states, groggy but awake.

General Davis enters the plane, and kneels down in front of Bill.

"Look, Bill, it's for the best. You need a break. You know there's nothing I can do about this, and I would if I could."

"But you know the truth, General. Vernon Presley is stealing my family—he's destroying my career. Damn it, General, don't let this happen. Please! I'm begging you."

General Davis looks down and directly into Bill's eyes.

"This is my life, General. My family is all I have. Please help me."

"It's over Bill. You did this to yourself."

The general gets up and walks out of the plane without looking back.

The next thing Bill remembers, he is waking up in a hospital bed at Walter Reed Medical Center in Washington DC. He sees his buddy Max sitting in the chair next to him.

"How ya feelin', Bill?"

"Better, I feel better," Bill replied. "Where the fuck am I, Max?"

"You're in the hospital in Walter Reed Medical Center in Washington DC, buddy. General Davis had you sent here." Max replies.

"General Davis, huh?" Bill said sarcastically. "What are you doing here, Max?"

"Davis had me transferred back to the States as well. I report to Ft. Jackson, South Carolina in a couple of days. I thought I'd come by before I have to report for duty to check on you. That's where you're going too after you get out of here."

"Says who?" Bill asked.

"The United States Army, that's who," Max replied. "As long as you quit telling everyone Vernon Presley stole your family."

"What the hell, Max? You of all people know it's true. Don't tell me you're on their side now?"

"Bill, if I were on their side, I'd still be in Germany. Anyway, I've always been on your side—you know that."

Max looks away for a moment.

"But Bill, they want you to stop. You've got to stop."

I'm sorry, Max, I can't do that. I don't have anything left but the truth and I'm stickin' to it. Vernon took everything else from me, but he can't take the truth of what really happened."

Max gets up from the chair and says, "Well, you've got a couple of months to think it over before you have to report, Bill."

"If I've got a couple of months, then I'm going to go see my sons."

"I'll see you in South Carolina, then Bill."

After 6 weeks in Walter Reed Medical Center's Psychiatric ward, Bill was released. He immediately made his way to Dee's sister's trailer to find his boys. He had to find a way to fix things with his family and get them back.

The Spoils of War

"The first and greatest victory is to conquer yourself; to be conquered by yourself is of all things most shameful and vile."

Plato

Bill knocked on the door of the trailer and Peggy answered.

"Bill, what are you doing here?" she said in surprise.

"Hi Peggy. The boys here?"

Upon hearing their father's voice, Billy, Ricky and David run to the door to greet him. They immediately salute him. Peggy lets him inside and Bill salutes them back.

"How are my little soldiers today?"

"Good, Daddy. Aunt Peggy's real nice to us," Billy answered.

"We miss you, Daddy. Where have you been?" Ricky asked.

Bill picks up little David and gives him a big hug.

"How's my David?"

"Good. I love you, Daddy."

David puts his arms around Bill's neck and stays there.

"Are you here to live with us?" Billy asks earnestly.

"No, son, just visiting you. I have to report for duty at Ft. Jackson in a few days," he said sadly.

"But Daddy, we miss you. Please stay," Ricky begged.

Bill puts David down and sits on the sofa with them.

"Now boys, you know I'm still in the Army, I can't just up and quit. It's my life and my job. You know that."

He hands them a wrapped package. "I thought you boys might like this." They open it and it's a book about tanks.

"We like it, we like it!" Billy shouts.

The boys lay down on the floor to read together.

"Want some coffee, Bill?" Peggy asks.

She is pours two cups at the dining room table.

"Sure, thanks Peggy. I hope them being here isn't too much of an imposition. I told Dee it would be too crowded."

"Aw, it's fine. Just one big happy family."

The phone rings at that moment and Peggy goes to answer it.

Bill drinks his coffee as he watches the boys read their book. He randomly peruses the papers on the dining room table waiting for Peggy to come back. One in particular catches his eye. The top of the page is stamped

"Vernon Presley" in gold foil type. He picks it up, reads:

"Dear Dee - The arrangements have all been made for the divorce. The papers are ready and just need signing. How should we contact Bill? I hear he's back in the States and out of Walter Reed.

Soon, you and I will be together again. Yours very truly, Vernon."

Bill sits stunned just as the door opens and Dee enters.

"Bill! What are you doing here?" Dee says in surprise.

She sets down a bag of groceries, then notices the letter he is holding. She grabs it from him.

"That's personal, you shouldn't have read that," she said sternly.

"Seems like you've got it all arranged then, Dee. Good thing I stopped by," he said angrily.

Peggy overhears what's happened and hurries the boys into their bedroom.

"Yes, it's all arranged. I'm divorcing you. It's for the best."

"Bill, you know I've always loved you. After all, you are the love of my life. But this is the way it has to be. It's a better life for the boys. Can't you understand that? Your drinking and fighting are bad for the boys. They deserve better."

"Dee, here's what I understand. You are a conniving, spineless woman who is out for Vernon's money. Period. It has nothing to do with the boys."

"Don't you insult me like that or you'll never see the boys again, do you hear me? This is their best shot at a good, normal life. That's what I'm concerned about."

Bill stands up as if to leave.

"They'll have a big house with a yard. They won't have to move every year. They'll get to have friends and won't be embarrassed that their dad is drunk all the time."

"So you did this whole thing for them, is that it?"

Dee nods.

"You know, you and Vernon deserve each other, that's for sure."

He heads out the door, not looking back. The boys yell at him through the screen, but he doesn't stop.

The Carnage of War

"Some people think that the truth can be hidden with a little cover-up and decoration. But as time goes by, what is true is revealed, and what is fake fades away."

Ismail Haniyeh

Dee, Vernon, and five Presley attorneys sit around the dining room table at The Graceland Mansion, Elvis's home in Memphis, TN. Bill stands, and all eyes are on the pen in Bill's shaky hand.

"Have we got a problem, Sergeant Stanley?" one of the attorney's asks.

Through the window, Bill sees his three sons, happy and playing in the backyard with Elvis. Expensive bikes and other toys are strewn all about the yard, and a brand new swing set gleams in the sun that he'd purchased especially for the boys.

"Actually, I do," Bill replied.

"I suggest you sign these papers if you ever want to see your sons again, Mr. Stanley," the attorney shot back.

"Stanley," Bill said firmly.

"Excuse me?" he said confused.

"I said Stanley god damn it. You've taken everything else from me, but you can't have my name. My sons will always be Stanley. Is that clear?" he shouted.

The lead attorney glances at Vernon, who nods his head.

"Fine," he said.

Bill looks back at the papers, signs his name, then pushes them across the table. He turns and walks out the back door and over to where his boys are playing. He calls them over and kneels in front of them. Elvis stays back.

"You're my little soldiers now, I'm not going to be able to live here with you."

He looks up at his oldest, Billy.

"Son, you take care of your brothers, you hear?"

"Yes, Daddy," he replied

"And all you boys, you mind your mother. Give her the respect she deserves. And mind Vernon too."

He pulls them even closer, burying his head in their clothing.

Dee watches from the window with tears

streaming down her face as she watches Bill say goodbye.

Elvis calls to Bill. They approach each other. "I'm so sorry all this has happened Sgt. Stanley."

"I know you are Elvis. You're a good boy, soldier."

"I promise you, Sgt. Stanley that I will take care of them."

"Thank you son, thank you. I'm going to hold you to that."

Bill comes back in through the side door and out to the driveway and Vernon follows him.

"I want you to have this, Bill," he said as he handed him a set of car keys.

"What are these?" Bill asked.

"The car. It's yours," he said as he dropped the keys into Bill's hand.

"And this should cover your outstanding bills. I know Dee overspent on you and I want to cover that."

He pulls an envelope of cash from his jacket pocket and hands it to Bill.

Bill knows the war has been won, and not by him.

"You know, the only reason I didn't beat the life out of you in Germany is because I gave her to you, understand? I sure as hell wouldn't keep someone who didn't want me," Bill spat out.

Vernon's expression is stone cold as Bill continues.

"You two deserve each other."

Bill starts to walk towards the light blue

Cadillac. He looks back one time.

"You take care of my boys or I will find you and beat the fucking life out of you, understand? Those boys deserve the best."

Vernon remains silent.

Bill gets in the car, starts the engine and drives off.

The next few days are a blur for Bill. He finds his way back to base in South Carolina and meets up with Max and starts drinking heavily.

"Bill, I'm telling you. You better ease up and let it go or your ass is gonna be out of Army altogether," Max warned him.

"Fuck 'em Max. I have given them 19 years of my life. What the hell else do they want?"

"Look Bill, I know it's been tough on you, but

you've only got six months left. Just act right, lay low and finish your career. You have your pension, and then you can start a new life."

Bill takes another sip of his drink.

"Right Max. Six months."

A captain who has had one too many drinks walks up to Max and Bill.

"Say fellow, rumor has it you traded your wife and kids for that Caddy out there," he said with a smirk.

Bill loses it, and turns and puts the Captain down with one punch to the mouth. Max grabs Bill and drags him out.

Within days, Bill stands in front of a judge trying to explain why yet again he was the subject of a court proceeding.

Soon after, Bill sits in his CO's office watching him fill out the paperwork on his desk.

The CO finishes writing and takes out an oversized stamp from the desk drawer and stamps the top of the papers--"

"DISCHARGE UNDER LESS THAN HONORABLE CIRCUMSTANCES AT THE RANK OF PRIVATE".

Three days later as Bill is nursing a drink in civilian clothing for the first time in 19 years, he sees a newspaper on the corner of the bar. He slides over and picks it up, and reads the headline:

"VERNON PRESLEY MARRIES DEE STANLEY IN A PRIVATE CEREMONY IN HUNTSVILLE, ALABAMA."

Epilogue

My mother's marriage to Vernon Presley on July 3, 1960 vindicated my father and proved his story--but it was too late. The damage was done.

In the span of just two years, this once proud military warrior and dedicated family man was reduced from combat hero to a broken individual--left with nothing more than heartbreak and the memory of the only battle he had ever lost.

I would spend the next 23 years since receiving my father's memoirs piecing together the events that cost him his family and the honor of his country.

It's become my personal crusade to right this

wrong and to restore the honor taken from him by the United States Army and Vernon Presley. Yes, my father's alcohol addiction was part of his tragic loss, but he fought valiantly for his country and deserved better.

The first step in my crusade came on June 6th of 1994 during the 50th anniversary of D-day. My friend Lamar Fike, Elvis' longtime friend and associate, took me to Normandy, France to commemorate those that lost their lives that fateful day, and those that bravely fought despite the odds.

As I stood on the beaches of Normandy that day, reliving my father's account from his memoirs, I felt his presence and could only imagine the carnage he and countless others must had experienced on this bloody beach 50 years ago. It was in that moment that I knew his story must be told.

The second step was to tell his story, and I've done so with this book. Now as I continue on, it is my hope that those who read this story will join me in convincing the Army to reverse my father's less than honorable discharge, reinstate his rank of Master Sergeant, and give him the military funeral that he was ultimately denied and all veterans deserve.

To me, Sgt. Bill Stanley is not only my father, but also the face of every forgotten soldier who deserves the honor and the respect of their country they dedicated their lives to defend.

"Honor those who deserve honor"

David E. Stanley

CPSIA information can be obtained
at www.ICGtesting.com
Printed in the USA
LVOW01s1502170916
505062LV00022B/679/P

9 780996 666725